Kingfisher
Science
Encyclopedia

General Editor: Catherine Headlam

5

HEREDITY ● LENS, OPTICAL

Kingfisher

KINGFISHER
an imprint of Larousse plc
Elsley House, 24–30 Great Titchfield Street
London W1P 7AD

First published by Kingfisher 1991
Reprinted 1993, 1995 (with revisions) (twice), 1997

British Library Cataloguing-in-Publication Data
A catalogue record for this book is available from the British Library

ISBN 1 85697 451 0

Typesetting: Tradespools Ltd, Frome,
Somerset
Printed in Spain

SAFETY CODE

Some science experiments can be dangerous. Ask an adult to help you with difficult hammering or cutting and any experiments that involve flames, hot liquids or chemicals. Do not forget to put out any flames and turn off the heat when you have finished. Good scientists avoid accidents.

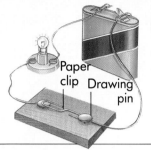
Paper clip Drawing pin

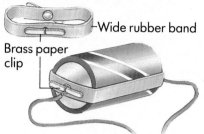
Wide rubber band
Brass paper clip

ELECTRICITY
- Never use mains electricity for experiments.
- Use batteries for all experiments that need electricity. Dispose of batteries carefully when they are used up and never heat them up or take them apart.

HEATING
- Tie back hair and be careful of loose clothes.
- Only heat small quantities of a substance.
- Always have an adult with you.
- Never heat any container with a top on it. Always point what you are heating away from you.
- Never hold something in your hands to heat it. Use a holder that does not conduct heat.

SAFE SOURCES OF HEAT
- Hot water from the tap or kettle is a good source of heat.
- A hair dryer can be used to dry things. Always take care when using electricity near water.

- For direct heat use a night light or short thick candle placed in sand in a metal tray.

Sand
Metal tray

CHEMICALS AND QUANTITIES
- Only use a small amount of any substance even if it is just salt or vinegar.
- Never taste or eat chemicals
- Clean up all spillages immediately, especially if on your skin.
- Wash your hands after using chemicals.
- Always ask an adult before using any substance; many cooking or cleaning substances used at home are quite powerful.
- Smell chemicals very carefully. Do not breathe in deeply any strong smells.
- Never handle chemicals with your bare hands. Use an old spoon and wash it very carefully after use.
- Label **all** chemicals.

SUN
- Never look directly at the Sun, especially when using a telescope or binoculars.

PLANTS AND ANIMALS
- Never pick wild flowers.
- Collect insects carefully so as not to harm them. Release them afterwards.
- Be careful of stinging insects.

SAFE CONTAINERS
- Use plastic containers if an experiment does not require heating or strong chemicals.
- Use heat-proof glass or metal containers if you are using heat.
- Avoid using ordinary glass as it may shatter.

CUTTING
- Use scissors rather than a knife whenever possible.
- When using a knife keep your fingers behind the cutting edge.
- Put what you are cutting on a board that will not slip and will prevent damage to the surface underneath.

Heredity

Heredity is the transfer of characteristics from one generation of organisms to the next. You will have seen that some children have features, such as hair colour, facial shape or mannerisms, which make them look just like one of the parents. Each of these features comes about because the fertilized EGG from which a new human develops carries two sets of instructions, one from each parent, that tell the egg what sort of features the new individual will have. These instructions are called genes. Although we inherit genes from each parent, some genes can over-rule others: they are said to be dominant. The effect of inherited genes depends on the interaction between genes from each parent.

Things like body weight, behaviour and fitness are not permanent features and are not inherited from your parents. They are the results of your life-style and environment. Things like the colour of your EYES and your BLOOD group are inherited and are with you for life.
See also CHROMOSOMES AND GENES; GENETICS.

Gregor Mendel (1822–1884)
Mendel was an Austrian monk and amateur botanist who pioneered the study of heredity. Through his experiments on pea plants he noticed patterns from one generation to the next, now known as Mendel's laws of heredity. The importance of his work was not recognized until after his death.

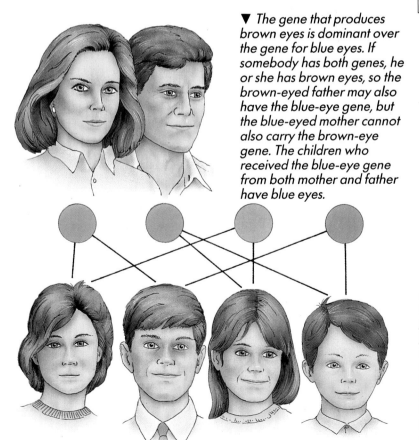

▼ The gene that produces brown eyes is dominant over the gene for blue eyes. If somebody has both genes, he or she has brown eyes, so the brown-eyed father may also have the blue-eye gene, but the blue-eyed mother cannot also carry the brown-eye gene. The children who received the blue-eye gene from both mother and father have blue eyes.

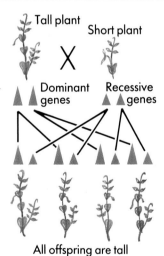

All offspring are tall

▲ Gregor Mendel did his experiments on heredity using pea plants. By crossing tall plants with short ones, he showed that tallness is dominant over shortness, because all the offspring were tall. But these plants still carry the gene for shortness and if they are interbred, one in four of their offspring will be short.

317

▲ *The aeoliphile, also known as Hero's turbine, was the first steam powered engine but the possibility of using it as a source of power does not seem to have occurred to Hero. Steam power remained undiscovered for another 1700 years. As well as the aeoliphile, Hero invented devices to open doors automatically.*

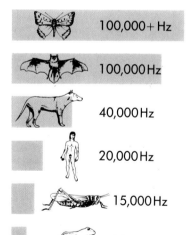

100,000+ Hz

100,000 Hz

40,000 Hz

20,000 Hz

15,000 Hz

10,000 Hz

▲ *The range of sounds heard by different species varies greatly. Humans have relatively poor hearing, and cannot hear sound frequencies above about 20,000 Hz. A bat's hearing is far better.*

318

Hero of Alexandria

Hero of Alexandria (1st century AD) was a Greek inventor and mathematician. He is famous for inventing the first steam-powered ENGINE and for his studies of GEOMETRY. His steam-powered engine, called an 'aeoliphile', was the earliest predecessor of the modern JET engine, although Hero built it as a toy. It was a rotating hollow metal ball with two nozzles on opposite sides pointing in opposite directions. When STEAM was passed into the ball, steam escaping from the nozzles made the ball spin on its shaft. He produced many formulae for calculating areas of different shapes, and one still called Hero's formula, for calculating the area of a triangle. His inventions included the first automatic vending machine which delivered a measured amount of holy water when a coin was put into a slot.

Herschel, William *See* Uranus

Hertz

The hertz (Hz) is the SI UNIT of FREQUENCY. One hertz corresponds to a vibration or wave that goes to and fro in one cycle every second, 10 Hz repeats 10 times a second, and so on. The kilohertz (kHz) corresponds to 1000 cycles per second and the megahertz (MHz) 1,000,000 cycles per second. We can hear sound frequencies between about 20 Hz and 20 kHz. Radio waves have frequencies of 200 kHz to 100 MHz.

The hertz is named after Heinrich Hertz who was the first to demonstrate the existence of RADIO waves.

Hertz, Heinrich Rudolph *See* Frequency

Hibernation

Hibernation is the deep sleep in which many small mammals pass the winter. Hibernating mammals include bats, hedgehogs and many rodents. They go to sleep mainly because there is not enough food around for them in the winter, but hibernation is not an ordinary sleep. The heartbeat and breathing rate slow right down and the body temperature falls almost to that of the surroundings. In this state the animals use hardly any energy and can survive on the food stored in their

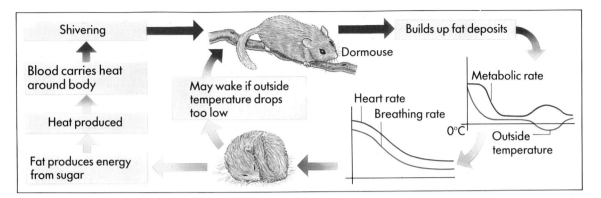

bodies. Some hibernators such as hamsters store food in their nests and wake up every now and then to eat it. Others, like bears, badgers and squirrels, go to sleep for days on end during the winter, but do not really hibernate because their body temperatures do not fall more than a few degrees below normal.

Amphibians and reptiles sleep through the winter, and so do many land-living insects and other invertebrates, but their sleep is not true hibernation. Many of them wake up on mild days in the winter and then drift back to sleep when it gets cold again.

▲ During hibernation, an animal's metabolism slowly consumes its body fat. The heat produced by the stored energy circulates in the blood and causes shivering. This keeps unused muscles toned up. If the air temperature drops to dangerous levels, the animal may wake up but, during severe winters, many hibernating animals die.

Hi-fi

Hi-fi is short for 'high fidelity'. It describes sound recording and playing equipment that satisfies a minimum standard for SOUND quality. Hi-fi equipment tries to reproduce sounds without distorting them. The sounds may include music and radio programmes.

▼ Most home hi-fi systems have the separate music sources stacked on top of each other and connected to the amplifier by internal wiring. CD decks and radio tuners often use illuminated numerical displays to indicate the CD track playing, or the frequency to which the radio is tuned.

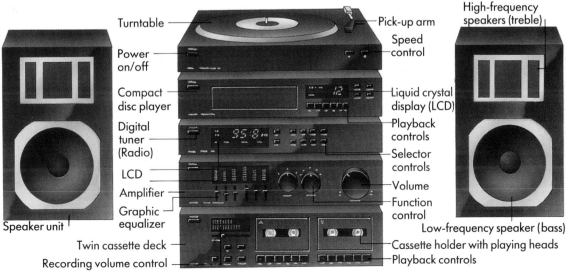

▲ *The first record players had to be operated by hand. Turning the handle wound up a spring that worked the turntable. The trumpet-shaped metal speaker gave very lo-fi sound.*

▲ *Hippocrates, the father of medicine, lived during the 'Golden Age' of ancient Greece (500–400 BC).*

Holograms are used to record very small changes in the size of objects. This is because they can record an object at many angles with great accuracy. Holograms taken of the same object at different times are used to measure minute changes in size. Scientists use them to study the growth of crystals or the build-up of dirt on old oil paintings.

Whether the system is a single unit or a number of separate units connected together by wires, it has a number of music or programme sources. Sources can include a tape CASSETTE RECORDER, a COMPACT DISC PLAYER, a RADIO tuner and maybe a RECORD player. They are all plugged into the AMPLIFIER's input sockets. The amplifier boosts the small electrical signals from the sources, and LOUDSPEAKERS turn the electrical signals into sounds. The amplifier also controls the volume and tone of the output. For STEREOPHONIC SOUND the original recording is made on two channels. They are amplified separately and fed to the two loudspeakers. Differences between the two channels make the sound more realistic than single-channel or mono sound reproduction.

Hippocrates

Hippocrates was an ancient Greek philosopher and physician who was born about 460 BC on the island of Kos. Little is known of his early life, but he travelled widely in Greece and the Middle East, teaching his theories of MEDICINE. He is often referred to as 'the father of medicine'. However, little is known about Hippocrates' own work, and most of the Hippocratic medicine we know about today was developed later by his followers. The most lasting influence of Hippocrates is the Hippocratic oath, which lays down a code of principles for the doctor, ensuring that the good of the patient is always the most important part of treatment.

History of Science

Ancient peoples knew the habits of animals and the powers of plants. But the Egyptians and Babylonians were the first to use science to explore nature and the Universe. Since then our knowledge has increased until in the last hundred years, science has gone from the atom and out into space, making greater strides than in all human history. *See* pages 322 to 325.

Hologram

A hologram is a three-dimensional (3-D) PHOTOGRAPH. A 3-D object has depth as well as length and breadth. To make a 3-D picture, a beam of LASER light is split into two separate beams. One part of the beam is aimed at the

Dennis Gabor (1906–1979)
Gabor was a Hungarian-born physicist who worked in Britain. He developed the theory behind holography during the 1940s, but actual holography became possible only after the laser was developed at the beginning of the 1960s. The powerful light of the laser allowed high-quality holograms to be made. Gabor eventually received the Nobel Prize for Physics in 1971.

object being photographed. It is then reflected back from the object onto a photographic plate or FILM. The other part of the beam is aimed directly at the photographic plate. Interference between the two beams produces a pattern on the plate that is not recognizable as a photograph. This pattern is the hologram.

When the hologram is lit by a laser beam, it produces a three-dimensional image of the original object. A viewer would be able to get a different view of the object as he or she walked around. In the future, holograms may be used in COMPUTER MEMORY systems.

It is much more difficult to produce a hologram than a photograph; any kind of vibration will interfere with the taking of a hologram. However, they are becoming more widely used and appear in advertisements and all kinds of decorative objects. Holograms are increasingly used in industry for measurement and inspection. A television that shows 3-D images using the principles of holography may soon be possible.

▲ *The photographic technique of holography makes these images, produced on a flat screen, appear in three dimensions.*

▼ *Holograms are made possible by the highly organized light of lasers. Splitting the laser beam enables the photographic plate to record a three-dimensional image.*

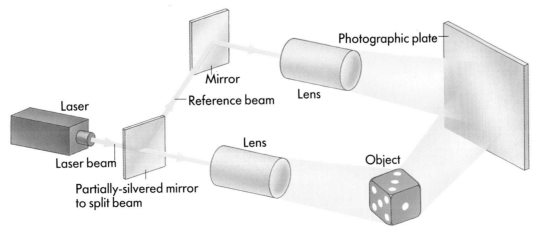

Photographic plate

Mirror

Reference beam

Lens

Laser

Lens

Laser beam

Object

Partially-silvered mirror to split beam

HISTORY OF SCIENCE

Last century, Mendel pioneered genetics, Darwin helped to develop the theory of evolution and Babbage made the first mechanical computer. As the century closed, scientists studied the atom and motion at the speed of light in space. Here Newton's rules did not apply: Einstein's theories of relativity and Planck's laws of quantum mechanics were needed. This century, nuclear power was born and the transistor and modern computer. The space age began: men stood on the Moon in 1969.

1000 BC–AD 500

First Olympic Games 776 BC
Roman conquest of Britain AD 43
Vesuvius erupts, destroying Pompeii AD 79

Hippocrates establishes profession of physician and begins to free medicine from superstition.
Chinese develop acupuncture.

Democritus states all matter is made of atoms, solid particles that cannot be divided.
Aristotle develops theory of four basic elements.

AD 500–1499

Marco Polo visits Asia 1271–95
Black Death kills 1 in 4 in Europe 1334–51
Columbus lands in the Americas 1492

Avicenna writes *The Canon of Medicine* – most important medical book for centuries (▼).

Alchemy comes to Europe from Arabia where its practice has given rise to first known book on chemistry.

5000 BC–1000 BC

Tutankhamen Pharaoh of Egypt c.1358
Israelites leave Egypt for Canaan c.1200

Egyptians devise the first calendar and use it to predict the Nile floods.
Babylonians predict solar and lunar eclipses.

The wheel (▲)
Glass (▲)
Bricks fired in kilns
Potter's wheel

Archimedes discovers the principle of levers and pulleys.

Ptolemy states the Earth is round and is the motionless centre of a revolving Universe.

Hindus devise a system of numerals.
Euclid writes his *Elements*. It will be used as a textbook for next 2000 years.

Water clocks c.650 BC
Abacus c.500 BC
Archimedes screw (▲) c.200 BC
Paper (for writing) c.100 BC

Roger Bacon experiments with lenses and discusses spectacles for the longsighted.
Leonardo da Vinci makes first observation of capillary action.

Chinese observe crab super-novas.

| 0 | 1 | 2 | 3 | 4 | 5 |
| 6 | 7 | 8 | 9 | 10 |

Algebra developed by the Arabs.
Arabs introduce Hindu numerals to Europe (▲).

Gunpowder c.1000
Magnetic compass c.1100
Spectacles c.1280
First gun c.1288
Printing press c.1440

1500–1599	1600–1699	1700–1799
Luther begins Reformation 1517 Ferdinand Magellan voyage of circumnavigation 1519–21 England defeats Spanish Armada 1588	Pilgrim fathers sail to America 1620 Louis XIV becomes King of France 1643 Plague kills 70,000 in England 1665	Cook discovers Australia 1770 American Declaration of Independence 1776 French revolution 1789
Vesalius's *On the Structure of the Human Body* – most accurate anatomy book (▼). John Gerard publishes his comprehensive *Herbal*.	Harvey discovers method of circulation of blood. Malpighi uses microscope to discover the structure of animals and plants.	Edward Jenner introduces smallpox vaccinations (▼). Linnaeus classifies 4400 animals and nearly 8000 plants.
	Boyle introduces modern idea of elements. 	 Lavoisier produces table of 31 chemical elements.
Galileo researches the laws governing falling bodies and pendulums. Stevinus conducts experiments for understanding gravity.	Newton makes discoveries about light and colour and the laws of gravity and motion (▲). Bacon advocates experiments for proof of scientific laws.	Euler works out mathematics of refraction of light. Benjamin Franklin performs his kite experiment, proving that lightning is electricity. Herschel discovers Uranus.
Copernicus puts forward the theory that the whole Universe circulates around the Sun (▼). Galileo first to use a telescope effectively and makes many new discoveries.	Kepler discovers planets have elliptical orbits – laws of planetary motion. Halley makes observations of comets. They later prove to be bodies with regular orbits (1705). (▶)	
	Calculus invented separately by Newton and Liebnitz. Napier develops logarithms. Pascal with Fermat develop the mathematics of probability.	
Leonardo da Vinci draws vertical take-off flying machine c.1500 Compound microscope 1590 Thermometer 1592	Telescope c. 1608–09 Submarine c.1620 Calculating machine c.1643 Steam pump 1698	Steam engine c.1712 Iron smelting c.1750 Spinning Jenny c.1764 Power loom c.1785

1800–1840	1841–1880	1881–1920
Napoleon invades Russia 1812 Battle of Waterloo 1815 Introduction of Penny Post in England 1840	Marx and Engels publish *Communist Manifesto* 1848 Lincoln becomes president of USA 1860 Suez Canal opened 1869	Amundsen reaches South Pole 1911 World War I 1914–18 Russian Revolution 1917
Lyell publishes his theory of Earth's development.	Darwin's observations during the voyage of HMS *Beagle* confirm Lyell's theories.	Wegener introduces Continental drift theory.
Schleiden and Schwann show that all plants and animals are made up of cells (▶).	Darwin publishes his *On the Origin of Species*. Lister begins antiseptic medicine and Pasteur shows microbes cause disease. Mendel's experiments reveal laws of inheritance of genes.	Freud's psychoanalysis experiments. Fleming discovers penicillin. Ehrlich begins treating disease with chemicals.
Dalton develops his atomic theory which is the basis of modern physics and chemistry. Davy isolates sodium and potassium using electrolysis.	Mendeleyev devises periodic table of elements. Bunsen and Kirchhoff design first spectroscope, discover caesium and rubidium with it.	Becquerel discovers radioactivity. Curies discover radioactivity of radium. Thomson discovers electrons.
Faraday conducts experiments with electricity and magnetism. Alessandro Volta invents first electric battery (▼).	Maxwell announces theory of electromagnetic waves. Joule measures amount of mechanical work required to produce an amount of heat.	Rutherford conducts nuclear physics experiments. Einstein presents his theory of relativity. Planck works on radiation.
		Ambrose Fleming produces first vacuum tube, which will be used in the development of radio and television.
Wallaston and Fraunhofer discover absorption lines in solar spectrum.	Adams and Leverrier pinpoint position of Neptune and Galle finds it with telescope (▲).	
Babbage develops program-mable analytical machine.	Möbius discovers a figure with only one side and one edge.	
Electric battery c.1800 Steam locomotive c.1804 Camera c.1822 Electromagnet c.1825 Telegraph c.1837	Safety pin c.1849 Passenger lift c.1852 Refrigerator 1858 Telephone 1875 Light bulb c.1879	Petrol engine car (▲) c.1885 Pneumatic tyre c.1888 Radio c.1895 Aeroplane c.1903 Bakelite c.1908

1921–1960	1961–1992	
World War II 1939–1945 First atomic bomb explodes 1945 Edmund Hillary first to climb Everest 1953	Assassination of J.F. Kennedy 1963 Chernobyl explosion 1986 Re-unification of East and West Germany 1990	◀ *Important world events that shaped the way people thought.* ▼ *Areas of scientific study.*
Discovery of paleomagnetism	First hole in ozone layer identified.	**EARTH SCIENCES** *See also* GEOLOGY; GEOGRAPHY; METEOROLOGY.
Salk produces polio vaccine. Watson and Crick reveal the structure of DNA (▶).	First human heart transplant. Smallpox wiped out by vaccination. Developments in genetic engineering.	**LIFE SCIENCES** *See also* BIOLOGY; BOTANY; GENETICS; MEDICINE; MICROBIOLOGY; VETERINARY MEDICINE.
		CHEMISTRY *See also* INORGANIC CHEMISTRY; ORGANIC CHEMISTRY.
Chadwick discovers neutrons. Bohr discovers structure of atom (▲).	Gell-Mann suggested existence of quarks. Quarks revealed.	**PHYSICS** *See also* ELECTRICITY; HEAT; LIGHT; NUCLEAR PHYSICS; SOUND.
Transistor invented. First integrated circuit is made, start of microelectronics.	Development of microchips and micro-computers revolutionized production of all kinds of machines.	**ELECTRONICS** *See also* COMPUTER.
Tombaugh discovers Pluto. Hubble discovers Universe is expanding.	Quasars observed. First Moon landings. Hawking developed his theory of black holes. Wrinkles in space confirm Black Hole theory.	**ASTRONOMY** *See also* SPACE EXPLORATION; STARS.
	A computer is used to solve a problem set by Archimedes.	**MATHEMATICS** *See also* NUMBERS; STATISTICS.
Electron microscope c.1939 Programmable electronic computer c.1943 Fibre optics c.1955 Artificial satellite (▲) c.1959	Laser c.1960 Silicon chip c.1961 Microprocessor (▶) c.1971 Space shuttle c.1981 Superconductors c.1987	**TECHNOLOGY**

HOMING

▲ *Pigeons' brains contain iron and this may act as a compass needle to help them find their way. They also have an excellent 'internal clock' which tells them the time at home. The position of the Sun or stars tells them the time where they are, and from this information they can calculate the direction to home. Near home, they find their way using familiar landmarks.*

People have been using homing pigeons for thousands of years. In ancient Greece, homing pigeons were used to carry the results of the Olympic Games to the different cities. Homing pigeons can fly at an average speed of 72 km/h over distances of up to 800 km.

▼ *Homing pigeons return.*

Homing

Homing is the ability of animals to find their way home. It is particularly important when animals have young waiting for food. Birds, bees and wasps use landmarks when close to their nests, but many birds can find their way across the sea and across land which they have never seen before. People who keep racing pigeons send the birds hundreds of miles away and then release them to see which one gets home first. Pigeons' brains contain iron and some scientists believe that the birds use this iron like compass needles to find their way. A Manx Shearwater taken from Britain to the United States in a closed box was back at its nest within 13 days of being released, having covered more than 4500 km at an average speed of about 440 km per day! Homing pigeons have been known to fly 970 km in a day. Pigeons two or three years old make the best racers but older birds are better at finding their way home in bad weather.

The homing mechanisms of guided MISSILES are different from those of animals. The missile is seeking the target. Detectors are linked to a COMPUTER which continuously adjusts the missile's flight path to keep it on course, even if the target is moving very rapidly.
See also MIGRATION.

Homogenization

Homogenization is a way of mixing substances that usually will not mix. If water and oil are stirred together they immediately separate again. Sometimes droplets of one can be spread through, or suspended in, the other. Milk is a suspension of FAT droplets in water. The fatty cream will always come to the top. Milk is homogenized by forcing it, under high PRESSURE, through a nozzle with

tiny holes in it to break up the fat into very much smaller droplets and spread them evenly. These much smaller droplets will remain suspended throughout the liquid so the milk will not separate.
See also EMULSION; MILK.

Hooke, Robert *See Elasticity*

Hormone

Hormones occur in both plants and animals. They are substances produced within the organism in very small quantities, which have powerful effects on organs and systems. In animals, most hormones are produced in endocrine GLANDS. Hormones are often referred to as 'chemical messengers', because of this controlling action in 'switching on' or 'switching off' the action of other parts of the body, including other glands.

The rapid GROWTH of the growing tip of a shoot is controlled by plant growth hormones. In mammals, hormones control growth and development, and play a very important role in sexual development and REPRODUCTION. Hormones are produced in the sex organs, kidneys, intestine, thyroid gland in the neck, and the pituitary and hypothalamus glands within the BRAIN. The human body produces 30 hormones, many of which play an important part in the health and development of the body. There is also a group of hormones called stress hormones and these are secreted in the presence of fear, injury or anger.

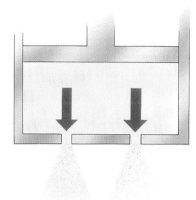

▲ *Forcing milk through tiny holes limits the size of individual fat droplets. Milk can then be stored without the fats separating out as a layer at the top of the milk.*

Homogeneous describes something that is the same throughout the whole of its volume. For instance a jelly is homogeneous but a currant bun is **heterogeneous** because its composition varies.

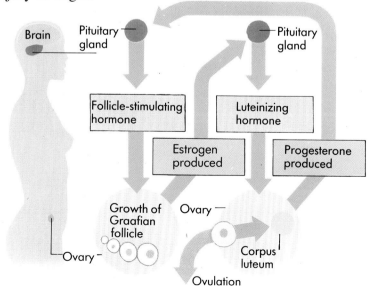

◄ *Several hormones from different sources may be involved during any single body process, such as the menstrual cycle. Two hormones produced by the pituitary gland – luteinizing hormone (LH) and follicle-stimulating hormone (FSH) – control the action of a woman's ovaries. FSH stimulates the growth of a Graafian follicle, producing an ovum. LH acts upon the corpus luteum releasing the ovum during ovulation. In turn the ovaries secrete two other hormones, oestrogen and progesterone, which influence the activity of the pituitary gland and regulate the menstrual cycle.*

Hormone	Source	Function
Prolactin	Pituitary	Controls milk supply and production of female sex hormones
Growth hormone	Pituitary	Works directly on the tissues to cause growth
Cortisol and corticosterone	Adrenal glands	Helps the body cope with pain and shock, and increases the level of glucose in the blood when needed. Also helps control fat levels in the body
Adrenaline and noradrenaline	Adrenal glands	Prepares the body when sudden activity is needed
Oestradiol and progesterone	Ovaries	Controls development of female sexual characteristics and growth
Testosterone	Testes	Controls development of male sexual characteristics and growth
Thyroxine	Thyroid	Speeds up chemical reactions in the body
Insulin	Pancreas	Controls sugar levels in the blood

What Horsepower?

James Watt invented the term horsepower in the late 1700s to measure power. One horsepower was a rate of doing work equal to 550 foot-pounds per second. A foot-pound was the work needed to lift or move one pound one foot.

▼ Although brake horsepower is an old engineering term, it is still used to compare different engines and vehicles.

Horsepower

Horsepower is a unit invented by the British engineer James Watt to measure the POWER output of an ENGINE. One horsepower is equivalent to the rate of working of an average horse. The power of a car engine is usually given in *brake horsepower*. This is a measure of the power output of the engine measured by a machine called a dynamometer. Before car engines were tested on dynamometers, their power in horsepower was calculated from the size and number of cylinders in the engine, which usually underestimated its power. Horsepower has gradually been replaced by the WATT as a measure of power. One horsepower is equivalent to 746 watts.

Type of vehicle	hp	Type of vehicle	hp
	1		300–500 bhp
	4		4500 bhp
	75–85 bhp		28,000 bhp
	80–105 bhp		

HORTICULTURE

Horticulture is the branch of crop-growing that deals with garden and greenhouse produce: flowers and vegetables and a certain amount of fruit. It is similar to agriculture in many ways, but usually carried out on a smaller scale and unlike agriculture only covers plants. Gardens existed thousands of years ago, but horticulture did not really become a science until the 20th century.

Horticulturalists produce many of the fruits and vegetables that we buy in the shops and they are also involved with the production of seeds and plants for sale to gardeners. A lot of this work involves finding out the best methods of harvesting seeds and storing them to make sure that they will grow properly. Much work is also done on breeding new and better varieties. Not all garden plants are grown from seeds. Horticulturalists propagate a lot of plants, especially trees and shrubs, from cuttings (small twigs cut from the plants and stuck in the ground or in pots of special soil). The twigs sprout roots after a few weeks and eventually grow into new plants. All are just like the parent plant, so the gardener knows exactly what variety he is buying at the nursery or garden centre. Apples and roses are more often propagated by grafting. Horticulturalists take special cuttings, called scions, from a desired variety and bind them to cut surfaces of strongly-growing young plants, called stocks, of another variety. The tissues unite and continue to grow, but everything springing from the scions is of the desired variety. It is possible to grow apple trees carrying several varieties of fruit by grafting several scions onto one sapling. Horticulture also involves recognizing the many pests that attack our garden plants and discovering ways to control them.

▲ The same plant may grow better in some places than others, depending on the climate and type of soil. Such variation is shown by these heads of maize (sweetcorn).

> Grafting is often used to produce new or hardier plants. A piece of one plant, the 'scion', is fitted into a cut made in the stem of another plant, the 'stock'. The two plants must be related: a piece of lemon tree can be grafted onto an orange tree, but not onto an elm tree. If a tomato plant is grafted to a potato stock the new plant will produce tomatoes, while the stock will continue producing potatoes!

SEE FOR YOURSELF
Planting seeds is not the only way to grow a new plant. During spring you can take a cutting from a tree or shrub. Choose a twig with a bud at the tip, and cut it diagonally with a pair of strong scissors or secateurs. Fill a small flower pot with a mixture of potting compost and soil, and plant your cutting (cut end down!) about 5 cm deep. Place the pot in a well-lit spot and keep the soil moist. After about 10 days, your cutting should have sprouted roots and begun to grow.

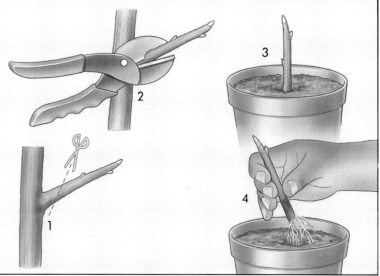

See also AGRICULTURE; BREEDING; CEREALS; FLOWERS; FRUIT; GENETICS; NATURAL SELECTION; SEEDS; SOIL; TRANSPLANTS.

► *The first diesel-powered hovercraft, the AP1-88, was launched on the Solent in March 1983.*

Christopher Cockerell (1910–)
Cockerell solved the problem of how to keep an air cushion underneath a hovercraft. Using part of a vacuum cleaner and old tins, he developed the principle of the air cushion. Cockerell put one tin inside another and blew air into the space between them. He weighed the result on kitchen scales and found that the air jet when compressed like this had three times the pressure of air just blown onto the scales.

Hovercraft

A hovercraft is a vehicle that floats on top of a cushion of AIR. Hovercraft can skim across land or water. The theory of hovercraft has been known since the 1870s, but the practical problems of building them were not solved until 1955. The main problem was how to stop the air cushion from simply blowing away from underneath the vehicle. The British engineer Christopher Cockerell solved this by blowing air, trapped in a ring or curtain, downwards all round the vehicle. This has the effect of holding the air cushion inside it. He built the first modern hovercraft, the SRN1, in 1958. Later models improved on the SRN1 by attaching flexible skirts all round the vehicle to help keep the air cushion in.

Hovercraft are propelled by large pusher propellers driven by the same ENGINES that drive the air cushion fans. Hovercrafts can reach a speed of 60 knots as they skim over the sea on a cushion of air.

The largest hovercraft now in use is the SRN4 Mark 3, which is over 56 m long and weighs 310 tonnes. It carries over 400 passengers and 60 cars.

► *On a hovercraft, most of the engine power maintains the cushion of air beneath the vehicle. A central fan draws in air from the atmosphere and forces it between the hull and the outer skirt. The air cushion reduces drag from the sea or land surface to a minimum; so that relatively little power is needed for actual propulsion.*

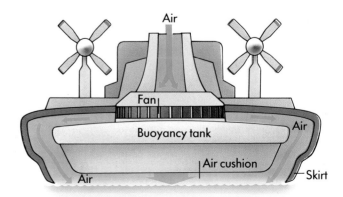

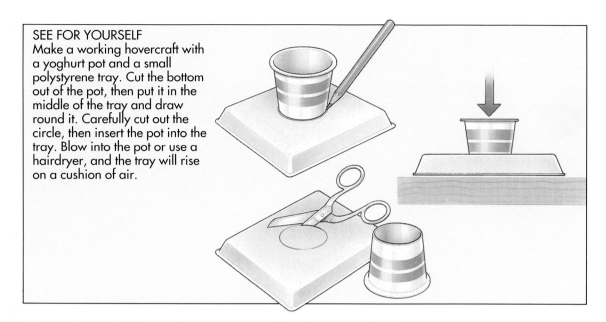

Hoyle, Fred *See Cosmology*

Hubble, Edwin *See Universe*

Humidifier

A humidifier is a device which adds moisture to dry AIR. Air conditioning systems used in offices and HEATING SYSTEMS can dry out the air too much to be comfortable for people. Breathing air that is too dry can irritate people's throats and noses. A humidifier works by trickling water over a material with a large surface area, enabling the maximum volume of water to come into contact with the dry air and evaporate into it. Alternatively, water may be sprayed directly into the air.

See also AIR CONDITIONING; EVAPORATION.

Home Humidifiers
People use humidifiers in the winter to help them feel more comfortable. Heated air from central heating systems is very dry and speeds up the evaporation of moisture from the skin. Humidifiers slow this process down and so reduce the cooling effect of evaporation, making people feel warmer at lower temperatures.

Humidity

Humidity is a measure of the water VAPOUR content of the ATMOSPHERE. It is measured with an instrument called a HYGROMETER. Absolute humidity is defined as the actual amount of water vapour in the AIR. It is the mass of water in a cubic metre of gas. Relative humidity is the RATIO of the water vapour present in the atmosphere to the amount of water vapour needed to saturate the air at the same TEMPERATURE and PRESSURE.

In clouds and fogs the air is saturated and its relative humidity is 100 percent. In desert areas it may be as low

If we sweat when the humidity is high, the sweat does not evaporate quickly and we feel uncomfortable and sticky. In dry, desert conditions (where the humidity is low), sweat evaporates.very quickly. An unwary traveller often does not realize how much liquid is lost as sweat, and so runs the risk of becoming dehydrated and losing too much vital salt.

SEE FOR YOURSELF
Make a hair hygrometer. Fix 2 paper clips into a block of soft wood. Glue a sliver of stiff paper into the eye of a needle and rest the needle on the paper clips so that the paper acts as a pointer. Wash a fairly long human hair in warm soapy water to remove the natural oil. When the hair is dry, pin one end to the block, and wind it once around the needle. Weight the end with a paper clip, and mark a scale on the block. The hair will stretch or contract in reaction to the humidity and cause the pointer to move along the scale.

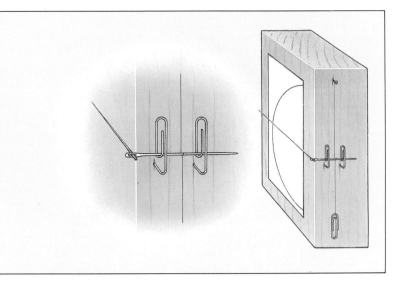

▶ When a mass of air is warmed by the Sun, it can hold more water vapour. As surface water evaporates, the water vapour is absorbed by the air and its humidity increases. Eventually the air cannot absorb any more water vapour. It becomes saturated, and evaporation ceases.

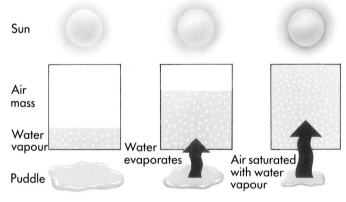

Sun

Air mass

Water vapour

Puddle

Water evaporates

Air saturated with water vapour

▼ The winds in a hurricane spiral around the eye, a central calm area of low pressure and light winds about 30 km in diameter.

as 10 percent. The relative humidity of air varies according to the temperature. Cold air can only hold a small amount of water, which is why dew forms in the early morning when the temperature is very low. As the air warms up it is able to hold more water.

Hurricane

A hurricane is a severe tropical storm in which the WIND reaches a maximum speed of more than 125 kilometres per hour or Force 12 on the Beaufort scale. The average wind speed is greater than 118 km/h.

A cyclonic tropical storm is usually called a hurricane when it occurs in the Caribbean area or around the northeastern coast of Australia. It can also be called a cyclone. The centre of a hurricane is known as the 'eye', and it usually stays out to sea but its high winds may cause destruction across nearby coastal lands, tearing up buildings or vehicles as the storm passes.

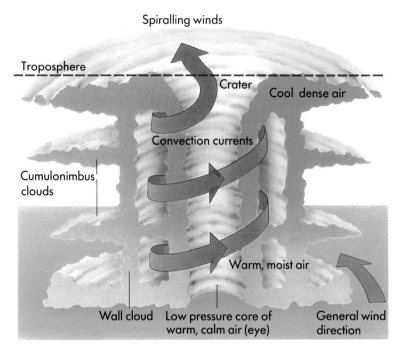

Spiralling winds

Troposphere

Crater

Cool dense air

Convection currents

Cumulonimbus clouds

Wall cloud

Warm, moist air

Low pressure core of warm, calm air (eye)

General wind direction

◄ *In the Northern Hemisphere, hurricane winds blow in an anti-clockwise direction, whereas in the Southern Hemisphere they blow clockwise. The winds reach their greatest speed (up to 250 km/h) within the wall of storm clouds surrounding the eye. As the winds spiral upwards, they create tunnels of clear air inside the cloud wall. In a typical cyclone or hurricane, the winds rise as high as the top of the troposphere before losing their force in the thin air of the upper atmosphere.*

Huygens, Christiaan *See* Light

Hybrid

This word is most often used to describe an animal or a plant whose parents belong to two different SPECIES. One of the best known examples is the mule, which results from the mating of a male donkey and a female horse. Mules are usually tough animals but, like nearly all animal hybrids, they are sterile. This means that they cannot have offspring themselves.

Many plant hybrids are fully fertile and many of our cultivated plants, including most of our CEREAL crops, are hybrids. Plants resulting from crossing two different varieties of the same species are also called hybrids and, like those between different species, they are often bigger and stronger than their parents. Producing plant hybrids can be a long process. Plants of the same species are inbred for several generations to give plants with pure heredity lines. These plants are then crossed with other inbred plants. Plant breeders work hard to produce hybrids of this kind in their search for bigger and better flowers and vegetables for the garden and the commercial market. Hybrids are also bred specially which have greater resistance to particular DISEASES. *See also* BREEDING; HORTICULTURE.

Horse

Donkey

Mule

▲ *A horse is strong, but needs high quality food. A donkey is much weaker, but can live on a poor diet. The mule is a hybrid of the two that combines their advantages, but it cannot breed.*

▶ *The wing flaps, under-carriage and landing gear of this Russian Mig 29 fighter are hydraulically controlled.*

▼ *Using pistons of different diameters within connected cylinders, as in a hydraulic jack, gives a mechanical advantage. A large movement of the small piston causes a smaller movement of the large piston. But the large piston acts with much greater force than the smaller one.*

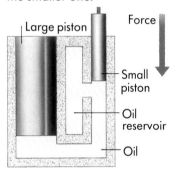
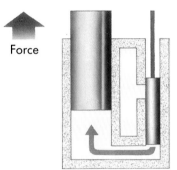

Hydraulics

Hydraulics describes the study of how FLUIDS behave. An understanding of hydraulics is very important in the design of harbours, docks and dams in which water may be flowing through rivers or canals, or may be enclosed in narrow channels or pipes.

Hydraulic machinery can be operated and POWER transmitted by using the PRESSURE of a LIQUID. If a pipe is filled with oil and fitted with a piston at each end, pushing one piston into the pipe forces the piston at the other end outwards. Power is transmitted from one end of the pipe to the other. Some excavators and cranes use this principle to lift heavy loads by the action of hydraulic rams. A hydraulic ram is a cylinder with a tight fitting piston, or ram. Oil pumped into one end of the cylinder forces the piston out of the other end. By attaching

SEE FOR YOURSELF

To make a hydraulic brake system, you will need 2 plastic syringes, some thin plastic tubing, a toy wheel and a piece of rubber brake pad from a bicycle. Fix the wheel to a wooden block, and tape one of the syringes to another block. Attach the brake pad to the end of this syringe. Then connect the syringes with the tubing, and fill them all with water. Spin the wheel with your finger, hold the other syringe in your hand, depress the plunger and the brake pad will stop the wheel.

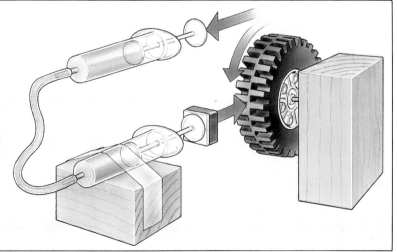

several hydraulic rams to a set of levers, loads can be raised and lowered very precisely. Some jacks used to raise cars to carry out repairs, work on hydraulic principles. Tipper trucks use hydraulic rams to tilt the back of the truck and tip out its load.

Hydrocarbons

Hydrocarbons are COMPOUNDS consisting of atoms of HYDROGEN and CARBON only. They form one of the most important classes of organic compounds. Hydrocarbons are found in PETROLEUM and NATURAL GAS and in coal tar, coal gas, paraffin, petrol and many other commercial petroleum products. The hydrocarbons in crude oil and natural gas provide the raw material from which plastics, solvents and many synthetic fibres and materials are made.

Aliphatic hydrocarbons have their main carbon atoms arranged in chains. They include compounds called alkanes or paraffins (such as methane, ethane and propane). *Aromatic hydrocarbons* are a small class in which the compounds are distinguished by a ring of six carbon atoms containing three double bonds. The best known aromatic is BENZENE, and the carbon rings are known as benzene rings. Hydrocarbons are different from CARBO-HYDRATES, which are organic compounds consisting of atoms of carbon, hydrogen and oxygen, and PROTEINS, which contain nitrogen as well.

Hydrochloric acid

Hydrochloric ACID is a highly dangerous, colourless LIQUID that fumes when exposed to the air, has an irritating smell, is very corrosive and can produce nasty burns. It is a solution of the gas hydrogen chloride dissolved in water. Concentrated hydrochloric acid contains three

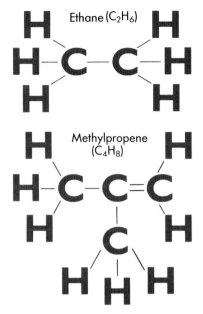

▲ *Ethane, formula C_2H_6, is a typical member of the alkane group of hydrocarbons. Methylpropene is one of the alkene group, and has the formula C_4H_8 with a double bond between two of its carbon atoms.*

▼ *The formula for hydrochloric acid.*

HCl

▼ *Hydrochloric acid is used to etch copper plates for printing. Before etching, the design is engraved into an acid-resistant coating such as wax. The plate is then inked before being pressed against the printing paper in the rollers.*

The etching process

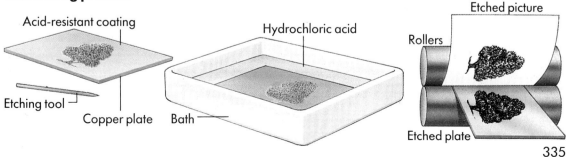

Acid-resistant coating

Hydrochloric acid

Etched picture

Rollers

Etching tool

Copper plate   Bath

Etched plate

▲ *Hydroelectric plants generate about 20 percent of the world's electricity.*

▼ *Water to drive the turbine is taken from a point midway up the dam so that the generators continue to operate even if the water level in the reservoir falls below normal. A spillway allows water to escape when the dam is full.*

parts of hydrogen chloride to seven parts of water. The hydrogen chloride is produced when the two gases HY-DROGEN and CHLORINE combine together or when sodium chloride (common salt) is treated with another acid, SUL-PHURIC ACID.

Hydrochloric acid reacts with bases to form SALTS called chlorides. It is used in industry to make other chemicals and in the processing of certain foods. The human stomach produces weak hydrochloric acid to aid the breakdown of foods during DIGESTION.

Hydroelectricity

Hydroelectricity is ELECTRICITY produced from falling water. Rain falling on high ground flows as rivers down to sea level. If a dam is built to stop the water flowing, a large lake, or reservoir, builds up behind it. In a hydro-electric power station, valves allow some of the water to escape from the dam through TURBINES. The fast-flowing water rotates the turbines which are connected to electricity GENERATORS. While the hydroelectric generator is working and the water flows out, the level of the reservoir falls. It is usually filled up by rain.

Some hydroelectric generators use a system called pumped storage to re-fill the reservoir. During the day,

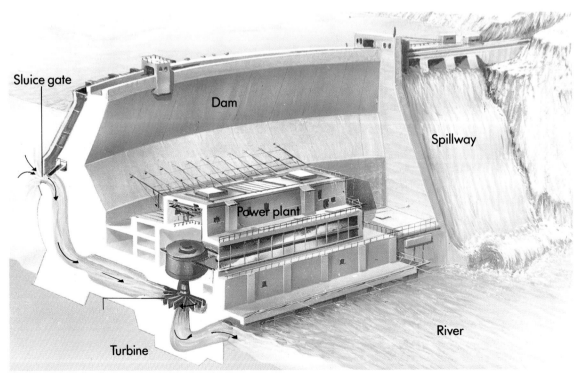

Sluice gate

Dam

Spillway

Power plant

River

Turbine

water flows from a high level reservoir through the turbines to a low level reservoir. At night, when electricity demand is low, the water is pumped from the low level to the high level reservoir. This ensures that POWER can be generated the next day. The largest pumped storage hydroelectric plant in Europe is at Dinorwic in Wales. In some mountainous countries such as Norway, most of the electricity is generated in this way.

Hydrofoil

A hydrofoil is a type of boat named after the underwater wings attached to the front and rear of its hull. When the boat moves slowly, it behaves like any other boat. When it accelerates to higher speeds, the flow of water over and around the underwater wings produces an upward FORCE called lift and the boat rises up in the water. Eventually, most of the hull is out of the water. The force called drag that resists the movement of objects through FLUIDS is therefore reduced and the boat can travel much faster. Jetfoils are propelled by water jets instead of propellers and can reach speeds of 43 knots, or 80 km/h. The first successful hydrofoil was developed by the Italian Enrico Forlanini in 1906. Alexander Graham BELL, the inventor of the TELEPHONE, developed the hydrofoil further.

Hydrogen

Hydrogen is a colourless, odourless, tasteless, non-poisonous GAS. It is the lightest, simplest and most plentiful ELEMENT in the Universe. The Sun's light and heat come from hydrogen atoms joining together in nuclear

Surface-piercing hydrofoil

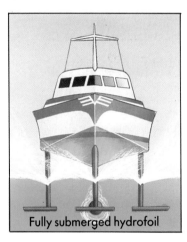

Fully submerged hydrofoil

▲ Hydrofoils can be classified according to the design of their underwater wings or foils. The more common surface-piercing types operate at an angle to the water, and gain some of their lift from the water surface. Fully submerged hydrofoils operate at much flatter angles, and gain lift in much the same way as an aeroplane wing in the air.

◀ This is a surface-piercing hydrofoil. When travelling at speed it uses the surface area of the foils for stability and control. This type of hydrofoil performs best on calm water such as lakes and rivers.

Henry Cavendish (1731–1810)
Cavendish was a British scientist who was both a chemist and a physicist. He is most famous for his work on the composition of air. Cavendish discovered the properties of hydrogen, and showed that air was a mixture of more than one gas. He was also the first to show that water is in fact a compound, and not an element.

fusion. It is found in a whole range of compounds, including ACIDS, HYDROXIDES, HYDROCARBONS, CARBO-HYDRATES and WATER. Hydrogen was used in ballooning, but because it readily bursts into flame, it caused many accidents and now balloonists use hot air or HELIUM. The ordinary hydrogen atom consists of a nucleus formed by one PROTON around which circles a single ELECTRON. This form, or ISOTOPE, of hydrogen is called protium. Two other isotopes exist, deuterium, a constituent of HEAVY WATER, and tritium. They are used to make HYDROGEN BOMBS.

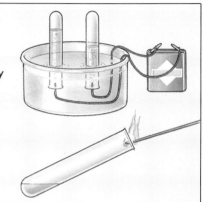

SEE FOR YOURSELF
Put some water in a dish and add a few drops of vinegar. Connect covered wires to the terminals of a large torch battery and put the bare ends in the water. Bubbles will start to form and these can be collected in tubes. Test the gases by holding a lit splint to the mouth of the tubes, the hydrogen will make a 'pop' and the oxygen will burn with a strong flame.

Nuclear fusion

Nuclear fission
Proton
Neutron

▲ A hydrogen bomb uses both fusion and fission. When the nuclei of deuterium and tritium fuse to form the helium nucleus (nuclear fusion), a highly energetic neutron is released. If the neutron subsequently strikes the much larger nucleus of a uranium atom, it splits the atom into two smaller nuclei (atomic fission), releasing energy.

Hydrogen bomb

The hydrogen bomb is the most powerful kind of nuclear weapon; it works by releasing a large amount of NUCLEAR ENERGY. The first nuclear weapons were made in the United States in 1943–1945; they used the ENERGY released when the nucleus of a heavy atom, such as URANIUM, splits in two. This is called nuclear fission; it releases particles called NEUTRONS which strike other heavy nuclei and make them split in their turn. This process is called a 'chain reaction'. It was this type of nuclear weapon, sometimes called an atom bomb, which was dropped on the Japanese cities of Hiroshima and Nagasaki in 1945; atom bombs have a power equivalent to many thousands of tonnes of ordinary explosive.

Later it was realized that more energy, equivalent to hundreds of millions of tonnes of ordinary explosive, would be released by the forcing together (or fusion) of two light atomic nuclei at very high speeds. This is the source of energy that is found in the Sun and other stars. The first hydrogen bombs were tested by the United States and the Soviet Union in 1953.

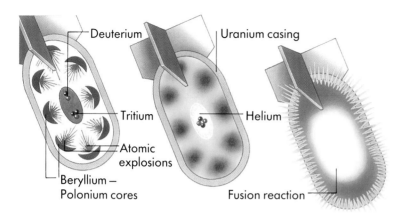

Deuterium — Uranium casing — Tritium — Helium — Atomic explosions — Beryllium — Polonium cores — Fusion reaction

◄ *The hydrogen bomb needs an atom bomb just to trigger it. The atomic explosion of beryllium-polonium cores creates the conditions under which heavy hydrogen (deuterium and tritium) fuse to form helium. Once the fusion reaction has started, it produces the energy which starts a second atomic explosion in the uranium casing. All three stages occur within a split-second.*

◄ *A test hydrogen bomb explosion caused this huge fireball. This explosion took place on an island in Bikini Atoll, a group of islands in the Pacific Ocean, on 21 May 1956.*

Robert Oppenheimer (1904–1967)
Oppenheimer was an American physicist, and is often described as the father of the atomic bomb. He was the senior scientist on the Manhattan Project which developed the atom bombs dropped on Japan at the end of the World War II. After the war, Oppenheimer argued for the peaceful use of nuclear power. He continued working as a physicist and did important work on black holes.

Andrei Sakharov (1921–1989)
Sakharov was a Soviet physicist who played a major role in the development of the Soviet hydrogen bomb. He later became a vocal campaigner for nuclear disarmament, and was labelled a dissident by the Soviet authorities and sent into internal exile. In 1975, Sakharov was awarded the Nobel Peace Prize. The more tolerant policies of the Soviet authorities allowed him to come out of exile in 1989. He died in Moscow shortly afterwards.

Hydrogen bonds

Hydrogen bonds are fairly weak chemical BONDS that hold together ATOMS, MOLECULES or IONS. An ice crystal is a giant network of water molecules held together by hydrogen bonds. They involve the interaction between certain chemical groups of atoms and other atoms that have a pair of non-bonding ELECTRONS.

When hydrogen combines with certain elements such as fluorine, nitrogen or oxygen, the hydrogen atom bonds with two atoms of the other element at the same time. The group can then bond to yet another atom by means of a hydrogen bond. Hydrogen bonding plays a major part in the way in which large molecules such as deoxyribonucleic acid (DNA) are put together. The spiral structures of PROTEINS, essential for all animal and plant life, are held together by hydrogen bonds.

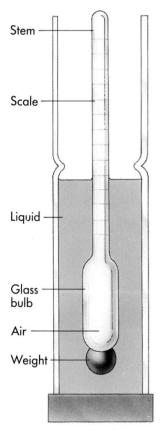

A hydrometer uses the principle of flotation. The hydrometer has a constant mass, and the depth at which it floats in a liquid is directly related to the density of that liquid.

340

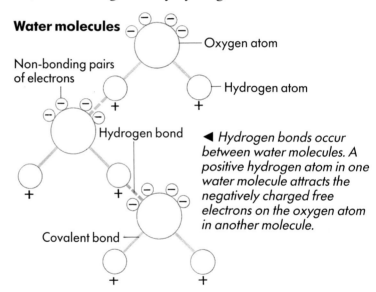

◀ Hydrogen bonds occur between water molecules. A positive hydrogen atom in one water molecule attracts the negatively charged free electrons on the oxygen atom in another molecule.

Hydrometer

A hydrometer is an instrument used to measure the relative DENSITY of a LIQUID. It is used to measure the strength of acid in car batteries or ANTIFREEZE solutions and often in home brewing. The hydrometer floats upright in the liquid so that the lower the relative density of the liquid, the deeper the hydrometer sinks, and the further up the graduated stem the liquid surface can be seen. Hydrometers are graduated so that the relative density of the liquid is measured compared to that of water which has a density of one.

Hydroponics

Hydroponics is a method of growing plants without SOIL. If you have ever grown mustard or cress seedlings on wet blotting paper you have done a bit of hydroponics yourself. Water and air can supply all the carbon, hydrogen and oxygen that plants need to make their food, but for healthy growth the plants need a number of other ELEMENTS, such as nitrogen, phosphorus and potassium. These elements are normally taken from the soil by the plants' roots, but if we give the plants the correct amount of chemicals dissolved in water, perfectly healthy plants will grow without any soil at all. Tomatoes and other greenhouse vegetables and fruit are often grown in trays of gravel with the carefully-calculated culture solution flowing through them.

See also PHOTOSYNTHESIS.

▲ *The roots of hydroponically-grown plants are wrapped in polythene. The plants receive nourishment from water containing artificial fertilizers.*

Hydroxides

A hydroxide is a COMPOUND of an ELEMENT (usually a metal or hydrogen) and a hydroxide group. Hydroxides are used to make detergents, drugs, paper and textiles. Sodium hydroxide (CAUSTIC SODA) and potassium hydroxide (caustic potash) are dangerous compounds that are used to attack grease. Dilute ammonium hydroxide is the household AMMONIA used for cleaning.

The hydroxide group (symbol –OH) is found in every alkali or base and in some organic compounds. Many alkalis, such as sodium hydroxide, form ionic solutions, which conduct ELECTRICITY. The solutions are bitter-tasting and soapy, and strong hydroxide solutions are corrosive and can burn the skin.

See also ACIDS AND BASES.

Hydroponics can be used to grow crops in places where there is no soil or the climate is unsuitable. It is used in the desert areas of Arizona, United States and the Persian Gulf. Scientists have been experimenting growing plants in the Arctic, at sea and in other places where plants could not normally grow.

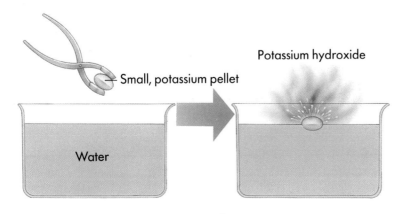

Small, potassium pellet

Potassium hydroxide

Water

◄ *When a small piece of potassium is dropped into water it reacts to form potassium hydroxide, and hydrogen gas is given off. The heat of the chemical reaction ignites the hydrogen, which burns with a bright lilac flame.*

341

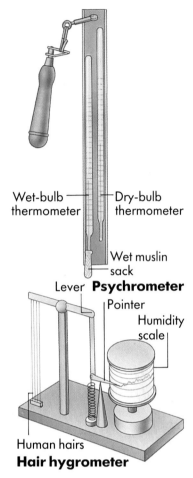

Wet-bulb thermometer — Dry-bulb thermometer

Wet muslin sack

Lever **Psychrometer**

Pointer

Humidity scale

Human hairs
Hair hygrometer

▲ *A wet and dry bulb hygrometer, or psychrometer, makes use of two separate measurements. A hair hygrometer gives a single direct reading based on the effects of humidity on human hair.*

▶ *When the fluid within a cell becomes hypertonic to the surrounding fluid, water molecules move out of the cell until a balance is achieved.*

Hygrometer

A hygrometer is an instrument used for measuring the HUMIDITY of AIR. Some hygrometers, called wet-bulb/dry-bulb hygrometers, are more refined versions of a simple thermometer with its bulb covered with wet muslin (wet-bulb). This is also known as a psychrometer.

The electrical RESISTANCE of the atmosphere varies with the amount of water VAPOUR in it. The more water there is in the air, the lower the air's resistance to ELECTRICITY. One type of hygrometer makes use of this property to measure humidity.

Hypertonic

A hypertonic SOLUTION is one in which the osmotic pressure is higher than that of another solution to which it is compared. Osmotic pressure is the PRESSURE that must by applied to a solution to stop the molecules of a liquid solvent passing into the solution through a membrane by OSMOSIS. The more concentrated a solution is, the higher the osmotic pressure. A hypertonic solution is therefore more concentrated than the one to which it is compared if their temperatures are the same.
See also HYPOTONIC; ISOTONIC.

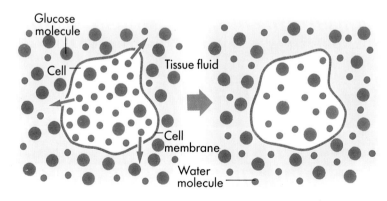

Glucose molecule

Cell

Tissue fluid

Cell membrane

Water molecule

Hypothermia

Hypothermia is a condition in which the body temperature of a warm-blooded animal drops so far below the normal level that it causes harm. If body HEAT is lost faster than it is generated, hypothermia results.

We shiver because the rapidly repeated muscular movements produce body heat. Cats and birds fluff themselves up when cold to increase the thickness of the

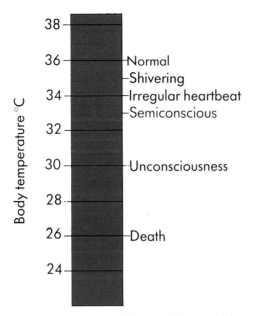

Body temperature °C

38
36 — Normal
— Shivering
34 — Irregular heartbeat
— Semiconscious
32
30 — Unconsciousness
28
26 — Death
24

◄ *The onset of hypothermia is quite slow, but once a person's body temperature has dropped by a few degrees the process speeds up.*

▲ *These marathon runners are wearing aluminium foil blankets to prevent them cooling down too fast. They have used up a lot of energy and need to conserve their body heat.*

insulating layer of air round them. Many old people cannot control their body temperature well, and when they get cold may not be aware of the signs of hypothermia, such as 'goose pimples' and shivering. If they are not warmed up quickly they become drowsy, lose consciousness and die.

Hypotonic

One FLUID is said to be hypotonic in relation to a second fluid if its CONCENTRATION is lower than the concentration of the second fluid. This is the opposite of HYPERTONIC.

In a living organism, when a fluid is hypotonic to a particular CELL, water molecules pass into the cell until the concentrations of the fluids outside and inside of the cell are evened out. The fluid becomes ISOTONIC to the cell when the osmotic pressure of the fluid equals the osmotic pressure of the cell.

See also HYPERTONIC; OSMOSIS.

There are a number of words that start with **hyper** and **hypo**. They have very different meanings.
Hyper means a greater than normal amount of something. In medicine hyperacidity means too much acid in the gastric juices.
Hypo means less than a normal amount of something. Hypothermia is a lower than normal body temperature.

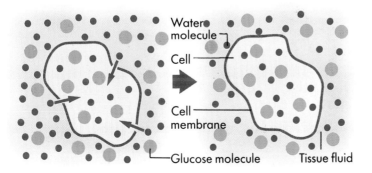

Water molecule
Cell
Cell membrane
Glucose molecule
Tissue fluid

◄ *When the fluid within a cell becomes hypotonic to the surroundings, water molecules are drawn into the cell until a balance is restored.*

343

▶ Over 75 percent of an iceberg lies below the water. Icebergs are a hazard to shipping so special patrols track them and report their positions to ships.

North Pole

Farthest extent of ice sheet

Today

▲ During the last Ice Age, the Arctic ice-cap was much larger than today. At the time of its greatest extent (about 100,000 years ago) it covered much of Europe and North America. The Antarctic ice-sheet underwent an equally dramatic change.

Ice

Ice is WATER in its SOLID, frozen state. Pure water freezes to ice at a temperature of 0°C (32°F). Water containing salt or other compounds freezes at a lower temperature. This is why salt is used to treat icy patches on roads and pavements. Unlike other liquids, as water freezes into ice it expands rather than contracts, increasing in volume by about 9 percent. If water freezes in pipes, the pipes may burst. Because it expands as it freezes, ice is

less dense and therefore lighter than water. This gives an iceberg its BUOYANCY and allows ice cubes to float on top of a glass of water.

Ice is still used to chill and preserve meat, fish, fruit and vegetables during storage or transit. It does this by lowering the temperature around the food and slowing down the action of destructive bacteria.

Ice Age

Ice Age is the name given to a period of the EARTH's geological history when the average temperature of the ATMOSPHERE fell over a large part of the globe to such an extent that ice sheets covered large areas of the Earth. Ice Ages are also known as glacial epochs. One important result of an Ice Age is a lowering of the sea level throughout the world as water turns to ice.

Within any Ice Age there are cold (glacial) periods and warmer (interglacial) periods. The Earth is passing through a warmer, interglacial period now, but 10,000 years ago, ice spread across wide areas of the northern hemisphere during what was a glacial period. There have been several Ice Ages during Eocene, Permian, Carboniferous, Cambrian, and Precambrian periods.

◄ *Granite rocks, formed underground but exposed by geological uplift and the forces of erosion. Granite is a very hard, weather-resistant rock.*

Igneous rocks

Igneous rocks are ROCKS, such as granite or basalt, which were originally molten magma or LAVA and which burst through the EARTH's crust. These rocks originate at fiery, white-hot temperatures.

As all igneous rocks cool, they tend to shrink and crack. Sometimes these cracks and joints take on particular shapes. If magma reaches the surface of the Earth still in a molten state, it may pour out as a lava. Sometimes, a lava may erupt under the sea and, as the sea water cools it, it takes on a characteristic form. Such lavas are usually called pillow lavas.

Granite is an example of an igneous rock which has cooled slowly. Its crystals have been able to grow to large size and so it is coarse grained. Basalt is an example of a fine-grained rock – it cooled quickly.

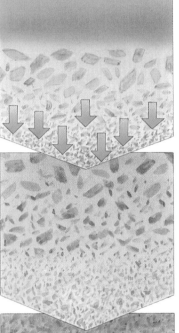

◄ *Liquid magma cools in a definite sequence (above), with rocks containing silicates of iron and magnesium (such as basalt and peridotite) sinking and solidifying first. Next to be formed are lighter rocks containing silicates of potassium, sodium, calcium and aluminium (feldspar and diorite). The remaining silica crystallizes as quartz (granite). The rate of cooling determines crystal size. Slow-cooling rocks have large crystals.*

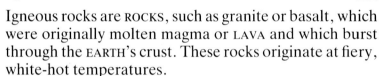

Granite

Diorite

Basalt

Peridotite

345

▼ Antibody cells are sometimes called memory cells. Once they have encountered an antigen, they will always recognize it. When such a cell encounters the same antigens **1**, it joins on to them **2** and immobilizes them until they are consumed by macrophages **3**. The cell then rapidly makes copies of itself **4** called plasma cells. These release antibodies into the bloodstream **5**, where they attach to antigens and attract macrophages **6**.

Immune system

An organism's immune system protects it from INFEC-TIONS. The main task of the human immune system is the production of ANTIBODIES. These are produced by the white BLOOD cells in response to infection. Antibodies destroy the bacteria and VIRUSES, or poisons produced by them called antigens, in our bodies. Once our bodies have learned to produce a particular antibody in response to a DISEASE, we can produce a lot quickly and this can prevent an infection developing: we have become immune to the disease. This is how VACCINATION works. The body is given harmless or dead disease organisms, so it can 'learn' to produce the antibody without risk of catching the disease. AIDS is dangerous because it damages the immune system, so the body cannot recognize other invading viruses or bacteria.

'Rejection' occurs when the body attacks organs which have been transplanted or grafted from another person or animal. This is because the immune system does not recognize the new tissue, and attacks it as an invader. Strong drugs are needed to prevent rejection.

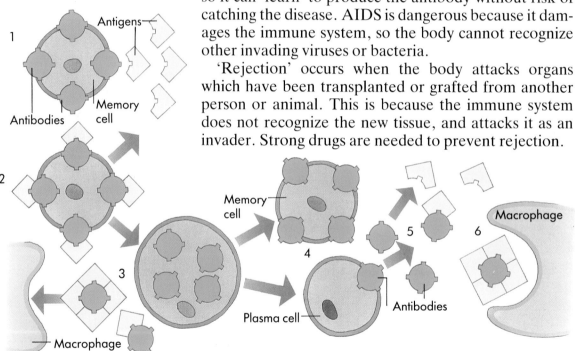

Antigens · Memory cell · Antibodies · Memory cell · Plasma cell · Antibodies · Macrophage

Most people carry the rhesus antigen. Those who have the rhesus antigen are designated RH+, those who do not are RH−. If an RH− woman is pregnant with an RH+ baby, leakage of the baby's blood to the mother causes the mother to produce antibodies. They do not develop fast enough to affect the baby she is carrying but may harm future children.

Implosion

An implosion is a sudden inrush of material. It is like an explosion except that the material is moving inwards instead of outwards. Implosions can happen because PRESSURE from outside pushes things into an empty space. Very large objects such as STARS can implode because the force of GRAVITY pulls everything towards the other parts. The implosion produces very dense material in the centre of the star which can become a NEUTRON STAR or a BLACK HOLE.

See also EXPLOSIVES.

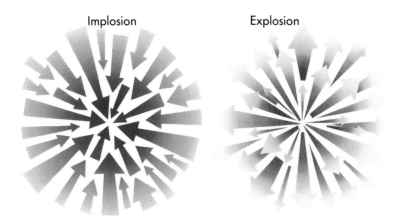

Implosion   Explosion

◄ All the force of an implosion is directed inwards towards the centre. Certain types of military explosive use the implosion principle. A small explosion creates a vacuum and the resulting implosion is much more destructive than the initial explosion.

Indicator, chemical

A chemical indicator is a substance that shows the level of acidity or alkalinity of a liquid. An indicator will be one colour in an acidic solution and a different one in an alkaline solution. In some indicators, the intensity of the colour indicates the strength of the acidity or alkalinity. Indicators play an important part in qualitative ANALYSIS. The best-known indicator is LITMUS which is derived from lichen and algae. An ACID solution will turn blue litmus red but will not affect the colour of red litmus. A solution containing a base, or alkali, will turn red litmus blue. Vinegar in water (an acid) will turn blue litmus paper red.

See also pH.

Universal indicator

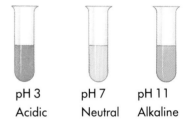

pH 3   pH 7   pH 11
Acidic   Neutral   Alkaline

Litmus paper

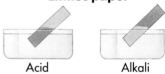

Acid   Alkali

Methyl Orange

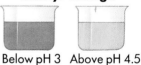

Below pH 3   Above pH 4.5

▲ Several different chemical indicators are used in laboratories. Litmus paper shows whether a liquid is acid or alkaline. Universal indicator enables the chemist to estimate the pH value of a solution fairly accurately. Methyl orange is useful only for acidic solutions. More sophisticated chemical indicators are used to measure other values, such as the amount of sugar in blood or urine.

SEE FOR YOURSELF
Red cabbage juice makes a simple chemical indicator. Chop up some leaves, and simmer them for 10–15 minutes. When the water has cooled, pour it into some clear glasses. If you add an acid, such as vinegar, the purple juice will turn pink. If you add some weak alkali, such as bicarbonate of soda, the cabbage juice will turn blue. Stronger alkalis, such as washing soda, will turn it green.

Joseph Henry (1797–1878)
The United States physicist Joseph Henry was one of the earliest pioneers of electricity. He discovered electromagnetic induction (the unit of inductance, the henry, is named after him) and invented an electric telegraph. Henry was appointed as the first director of the Smithsonian Institution in Washington.

Inductance, self and magnetic

Inductance is a measure of the opposition to the change of current in a electrical CIRCUIT. Self-inductance occurs when the magnetic field in an electrical circuit changes. Magnetic induction is the process by which an electric current is made to flow in a circuit because a magnetic field has moved.

Hans Oersted showed that there was a link between ELECTRICITY and MAGNETISM when he showed that an electric current can produce a magnetic field. Michael FARADAY in Britain and Joseph Henry in the United States developed this idea further when they showed that a magnetic field could produce an electric current. If a wire is made into a complete circuit and is moved through a magnetic field, or the circuit remains still and the magnetic field moves, then the voltage is induced in the circuit and electricity flows. When the magnetic field and wire circuit are both stationary, no electricity flows in the wire circuit. This idea led to the development of the generator used in power stations to produce electric-

▼ Moving a magnet through a coil of wire induces an electric current in the wire. The direction of the current flow depends on the direction of movement. Electrical generators use rotary movement and spin a coil within a magnetic field.

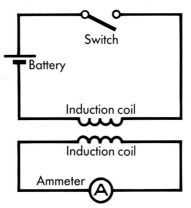

◀ Because of inductance, a change in the electric current flowing in one circuit can cause a current to flow in a different circuit nearby. When the switch is closed in the upper circuit, current from the battery flows through the coil. This causes a changing magnetic field which links with the coil in the lower circuit. The ammeter shows that a current flows briefly.

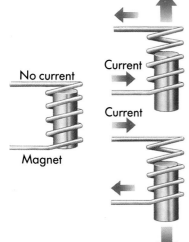

ity. In a power station coils of wire spin rapidly in a magnetic field and this induces an electric current in the moving coils. The electricity is then sent to our homes. When the coils stop spinning, the induced voltage ceases too. The dynamo which runs the lights on a bicycle is just a smaller version of a power station, because it too depends on the movement of the magnetic field in relation to the electric circuit to induce a voltage which then lights up the lights.

The SI UNIT of inductance is the henry (H). A potential difference of one volt will appear across a circuit with a self-inductance of one henry when the current changes by one AMPERE per second.

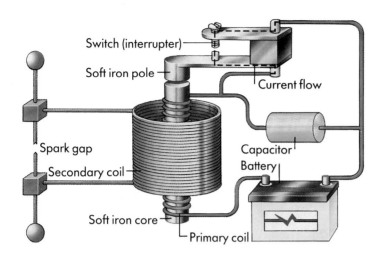

Switch (interrupter)
Soft iron pole
Current flow
Spark gap
Secondary coil
Capacitor
Battery
Soft iron core
Primary coil

◀ *In the ignition circuit of a car engine, the switch is initially operated by the capacitor which discharges at very brief intervals. Interrupting the low-voltage current through the primary coil induces a high-voltage current in the secondary coil. This causes sparks to arc across the spark gap, igniting the fuel/air mixture in the combustion chamber. When the engine is running normally, the timing of the interrupter switch is controlled by the speed of the engine.*

Induction coil

An induction coil is a kind of TRANSFORMER that produces pulses of high-voltage electric current from lower voltage current. It consists of a primary coil of wire with quite a few turns and a secondary coil of wire with a much larger number of turns in it. If an electric current in the primary coil is interrupted repeatedly, it creates a changing magnetic field around both coils. Induction causes a very large voltage in the secondary coil.

Induction coils are used to produce short bursts of high voltages, particularly in INTERNAL COMBUSTION ENGINES in vehicles. Induction coils have a current driven through them by the relatively low voltage of the BATTERY and then produce a large voltage across the terminals of the spark plug. This voltage produces the spark which ignites the FUEL and air in the cylinder.

Cotton gin

Industrial Revolution

The Industrial Revolution was a period of great change in Britain in the 18th century. Before then most goods were made by hand and most people worked in the countryside. In the 18th century there were a number of inventions and developments that changed this. The STEAM ENGINE could operate machinery more quickly and reliably than the water wheels and mills that drove them before. Improvements in spinning and weaving MACHINES followed. The use of steam engines and more powerful machines made the COAL and iron industries the most important in the country. Wood was replaced by IRON AND STEEL as a material for making things.

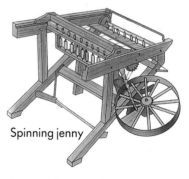

Spinning jenny

▲ *Machines used in the cotton industry were among the first to be adapted to steam power. Removing seeds and impurities from the fibres could be done in hand-turned gins, but the externally powered spinning jenny enabled skilled workers to be many times more productive.*

349

▶ *The spinning mule was introduced by Samuel Crompton in 1779. It produced very fine, uniform yarn.*

▼ *The weaving industry saw some of the first factory automation with the Jacquard loom. A series of cards containing a coded sequence of holes are used to control the weaving of elaborate patterns in cloth and carpets.*

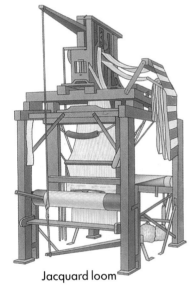

Jacquard loom

All over the country, factories were built for the new machines. They attracted workers who had lived in the countryside. This led to the growth of large industrial towns where living conditions were poor. Houses for the factory workers were packed close together and clean water supplies and proper drainage were rare. Health did not improve until the middle of the 19th century.

The increasing quantities of goods being made in factories needed better transport systems to carry them to shops and industries. The railway network that spread across the country in the 19th century helped, as did the CONSTRUCTION of new roads and bridges. Steam engines propelled ships that no longer relied on the wind.

Inertia

Inertia is the name given to the tendency of an object to stay still or to move steadily in a straight line unless some FORCE pushes it and makes it behave in a different way. The greater an object's inertia, the larger is the force

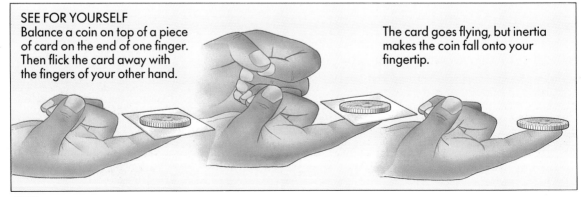

SEE FOR YOURSELF
Balance a coin on top of a piece of card on the end of one finger. Then flick the card away with the fingers of your other hand.

The card goes flying, but inertia makes the coin fall onto your fingertip.

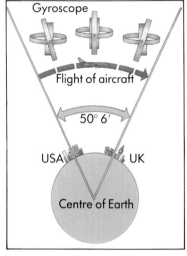

◄ Inertia keeps these dummy passengers moving forward when the test car stops suddenly. It shows how important seat-belts are in restraining these forces by stopping people from being thrown forward.

that is necessary to make it ACCELERATE (that is, move from rest or change the speed or direction of its motion). The amount of material (or MASS) which is present in an object determines how much inertia it has.

It was Isaac NEWTON who first realized that a force was needed to overcome inertia and make an object accelerate or decelerate.

Inertial guidance

Inertial guidance is a way of keeping a rocket, submarine, ship or aircraft on a particular course. In an inertial guidance system, a platform or table is kept stationary by three spinning, or LASER, GYROSCOPES, one for each of the three directions: up/down, forwards/backwards and left/right. Whatever way the vehicle turns or changes speed, the gyroscopes resist these movements and keep the table steady. Devices called accelerometers measure the FORCES trying to move the table. Signals from the accelerometers are fed to a COMPUTER, which uses them to calculate how far the vehicle has moved and in which direction. If it has strayed off course, the computer calculates the correction and produces the electrical signals to operate the vehicle's steering gear to bring it back on course.

▲ An automatic pilot tracks an aircraft's progress by reference to the angle of the gyroscopes. An angular difference of 50° 6', equates to the 3,006 nautical miles between London and New York.

▼ Three gyroscopes provide the computer with information in three dimensions.

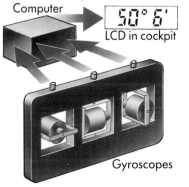

Infection

Infection takes place when an organism is invaded by harmful bacteria and VIRUSES which multiply in the organism and cause damage. These invaders can enter the organism through many routes. In humans, they may

▶ *A cut tomato left exposed to the air soon goes mouldy. This shows that germs and other infective organisms are in the air all the time, and attack anything they can live on. Most of the patches of mould are caused by varieties of fungus.*

▲ *We are surrounded by possible sources of infection: household pests often carry dangerous microorganisms, some diseases are transmitted by close contact between people, and others arise from eating food that is not fresh.*

enter through the mouth when we eat contaminated food or dirty water, or they can be inhaled through the lungs. An important route of infection is through the skin, for example, an insect bite or a dirty cut. There are also some infections passed on during sexual activity with an infected person. Infection can be prevented by avoiding close contact with a sick person and by proper hygiene and the use of disinfectants to keep things clean.

Infinity

Infinity is a number, quantity, or distance that is so large it cannot be counted or measured. In GEOMETRY, infinity is an unreachable, distant point. The idea of infinity helps distinguish between two classes of sets. One type of set consists of a countable number of members. For example, the days of the week make up a finite set of seven members. All the positive whole numbers (1, 2, 3, 4, ...) make up an infinite set because they go on for ever. Infinity is where the numbers finally run out, but this point can never be reached.

Parallel Light

The Sun is not an infinite distance from the Earth (it is 150 million km away), but for experiments sunlight is considered to travel in parallel lines as if from infinity.

  Sun

Information technology

Information technology describes the storage, processing and transmission of information by computerized systems. In a world increasingly dependent on science and technology, fast and easy access to accurate information is very important. The development of inexpensive COMPUTERS and TELECOMMUNICATIONS made this possible in the 1980s. Information about all sorts of research and technology projects is stored in computers all over the world. The TELEPHONE network provides a global COMMUNICATIONS network, called the Internet, capable of linking these computers together. Information stored in one computer can be sent to another computer anywhere in the world, provided that both are connected to a telephone line.

Information technology enables someone with a small home computer to look through a library of information, called a computer database, stored in a much bigger computer somewhere else in the world. Some shops, especially supermarkets, use information technology in monitoring their stock levels. The shop's computer detects when stocks run low and automatically places a new order. Goods are paid for in some shops by wiping a plastic card through a slot in a card reader. It reads a magnetic stripe on the card, contacts the card owner's bank computer by telephone and automatically deducts the amount spent from the card owner's account.

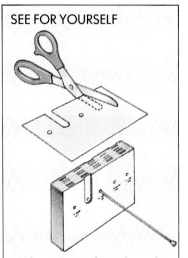

SEE FOR YOURSELF

Make a series of punch cards about your friends. Ask them each the same series of questions about themselves. The questions must have yes/no answers, e.g. are you more than 1.5 m tall? Mark the answers in the same place on each card. Cut a hole for a yes, and a wide groove for a no. To find out how many of your friends are over 1.5 m tall, push a knitting needle through the hole for that question. The cards with the answer 'yes' will be threaded onto the needle, while the 'no' cards will fall away.

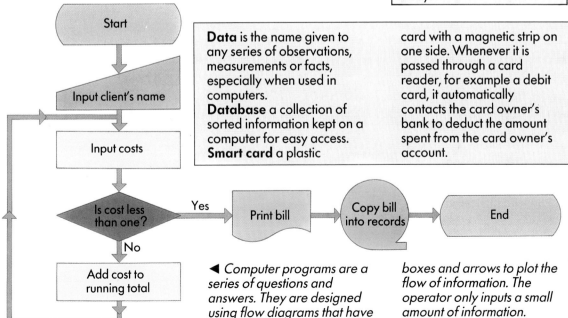

Data is the name given to any series of observations, measurements or facts, especially when used in computers.
Database a collection of sorted information kept on a computer for easy access.
Smart card a plastic card with a magnetic strip on one side. Whenever it is passed through a card reader, for example a debit card, it automatically contacts the card owner's bank to deduct the amount spent from the card owner's account.

◄ *Computer programs are a series of questions and answers. They are designed using flow diagrams that have boxes and arrows to plot the flow of information. The operator only inputs a small amount of information.*

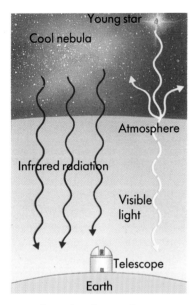

Young star
Cool nebula
Atmosphere
Infrared radiation
Visible light
Telescope
Earth

▲ *Infrared radiation from distant objects in space can penetrate the Earth's atmosphere more easily than visible light, much of which is reflected. Astronomers use infrared photography to observe these objects, because the human eye sees only visible light.*

▶ *Infrared photography shows one aircraft has already departed. The normally invisible heat imprint left behind, the thermal shadow, shows up on the tarmac.*

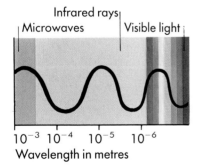

Infrared rays
Microwaves
Visible light

10^{-3} 10^{-4} 10^{-5} 10^{-6}
Wavelength in metres

▲ *Infrared radiation lies close to the visible band of the electromagnetic spectrum. The wavelength of infrared energy is greater than that of visible light, but shorter than microwaves.*

Infrared astronomy

Infrared astronomy is a branch of ASTRONOMY which studies the INFRARED RADIATION from the STARS, PLANETS and other bodies. Infrared wavelengths are longer than the WAVELENGTHS of visible light and shorter than radio wavelengths. Cooler objects send out less infrared radiation than hot ones do. Infrared radiation can also pass through 'dusty' regions of the Galaxy, revealing otherwise invisible objects.

Infrared astronomers have detected very young stars that are not yet glowing brightly.

Infrared photography

Infrared PHOTOGRAPHY is used to obtain important information about crops, valuable MINERALS, forests and POLLUTION by detecting the amount of heat they give out.

Hot materials send out ELECTROMAGNETIC RADIATION just beyond the red end of the range of colours that the human eye can see. It is therefore called INFRARED RADIATION. Chemicals polluting the sea soak up heat differently from the surrounding water and show up against the colder water in an infrared photograph as do rocks containing valuable minerals.

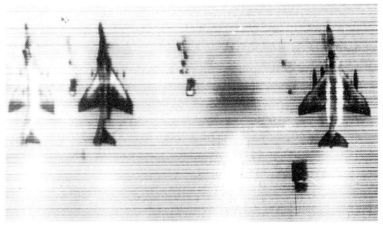

Infrared radiation

Infrared radiation, often called heat rays, is ELECTROMAGNETIC RADIATION which is similar to LIGHT but which lies beyond the red end of the visible SPECTRUM. The different colours of light look different from one another because the electromagnetic radiation which makes them up has different FREQUENCIES and WAVELENGTHS; infrared radiation has longer wavelengths and lower frequencies than visible light. Its wavelength can be between 800 nm (800 millionths of a millimetre) and a few tenths of a millimetre.

Infrared radiation allows us to 'see' objects which do not transmit light and are therefore invisible. For example, people give out infrared radiation, so they can be detected at night or in a building which has been shattered by an earthquake.

See also INFRARED ASTRONOMY; INFRARED PHOTOGRAPHY.

Inheritance *See* Heredity

Injection moulding

Injection moulding is one way of making objects from PLASTIC. A mould is made in two halves which are clamped together. Plastic granules are heated to change them from a solid into a thick liquid. The hot molten plastic is then forced or injected into the mould.

▲ *Injection moulding is often used in the manufacture of plastic pipes and pipe joints.*

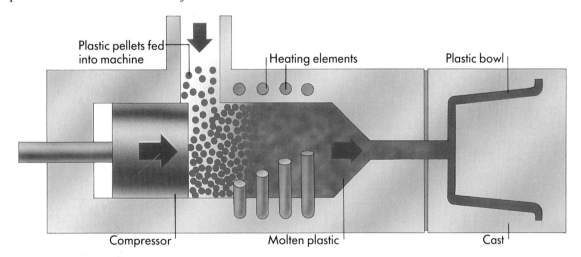

Plastic pellets fed into machine — Heating elements — Plastic bowl

Compressor — Molten plastic — Cast

Several objects can be moulded at the same time by linking their separate moulds by channels along which the molten plastic can flow. The plastic soon cools and sets. The mould is split apart and the plastic parts can be pulled out. On many plastic objects you can see the point where the plastic was injected into the mould as a small bump on the bottom of the object.

See also EXTRUSION.

▲ *Injection moulding leaves distinctive traces on objects that have been produced by this method. A plastic washing-up bowl usually has a faint seam around its circumference, which shows the line where the two halves of the mould met. In the centre of the underside, a circular bump indicates where the molten plastic was injected.*

Inoculation *See* Vaccination

INORGANIC CHEMISTRY

Inorganic chemistry is a major branch of chemistry that deals with the properties and reactions of substances that do not contain carbon atoms bonded to other carbon atoms. Inorganic chemistry covers the individual elements and all the simpler compounds such as oxides, mineral acids (nitric, sulphuric or hydrochloric acid), bases and salts such as sodium chloride (common salt), copper sulphate, sodium nitrate, and so on. It also embraces the study of metals. Some elements are very similar and react progressively strongly with particular compounds. Some carbon compounds, the carbonates and oxides, are treated as part of inorganic chemistry.

The physical properties of these various elements and compounds, such as their crystal structure, is studied separately as *physical chemistry*.

The history of chemistry prior to 1828 is really the story of inorganic chemistry. It concerns the discovery of certain elements such as mercury, sulphur, gold, silver and copper in ancient times and the isolation of others, such as hydrogen, sodium and potassium and the preparation and identification of simple compounds such as carbon dioxide in the 1700s and 1800s. More recently inorganic chemistry has been distinguished from organic chemistry, which deals with the substances and reactions of living matter, such as carbohydrates, hydrocarbons, proteins and amino acids, all of which contain carbon.

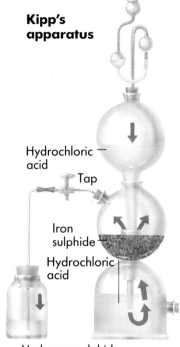

Kipp's apparatus

Hydrochloric acid

Tap

Iron sulphide

Hydrochloric acid

Hydrogen sulphide

▲ *Kipp's apparatus was used to produce a gas by reacting a liquid with a solid. The action of hydrochloric acid on iron sulphide makes hydrogen sulphide. The apparatus incorporates a safety device. Closing the tap creates gas pressure in the middle flask, which prevents the acid from dripping down.*

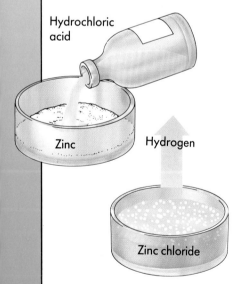

Hydrochloric acid

Zinc

Hydrogen

Zinc chloride

▲ *Inorganic chemistry deals with basic chemical reactions such as the one that takes place between zinc and hydrochloric acid to produce zinc chloride and hydrogen gas.*

Milestones in Inorganic Chemistry
1828 Friedrich Wöhler makes the first synthetic organic substance from inorganic compounds.
1856 The first synthetic dye made by William Perkin.
1895 August Kekulé's structure of benzene.
1910 Synthetic ammonia produced by Fritz Haber.
1950s Research into structure of DNA.

▶ *The fountain experiment demonstrates the solubility of ammonia in water. As the ammonia dissolves, a partial vacuum is created in the upper flask, making a fountain. Adding red litmus to the water creates a fountain that changes colour.*

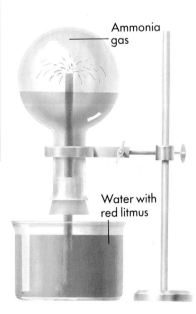

Ammonia gas

Water with red litmus

See also ATOM; BOND, CHEMICAL; CHEMISTRY; COMPOUND; ELEMENT, CHEMICAL; LABORATORY; ORGANIC CHEMISTRY; PERIODIC TABLE.

Insecticide *See* Pesticide

Instinct

A baby spider can spin a perfect web without having to learn how to do it. We call this kind of inborn behaviour an instinct. Spiders of the same SPECIES all build in the same way because they are born with the same instinct, just as they are born the same shape and colour.

Biologists once thought that all animal BEHAVIOUR was instinctive, but as they studied the animals in more detail they discovered that this is not true. Although animals have a lot of instinctive ability, their reactions are almost always modified by experience or LEARNING. Most animal behaviour is therefore a mixture of inborn (instinctive) and learned behaviour. Young birds, for example, know how to sing, but they have to learn the right songs from their parents. Biologists and psychologists are generally interested in overall behaviour not just instinctive patterns. In human beings learning seems to be more important than instinct in determining final behaviour patterns.

▲ Gull chicks instinctively peck towards the red spot on a parent's beak, because 'beak' means 'food' for hungry chicks. A newly hatched chick will peck at any similar combination of colours.

◄ The female cuckoo lays her eggs in other birds' nests. When the egg hatches the cuckoo will instinctively knock all the other eggs out of the nest. The cuckoo never knows its parents but as it grows it will behave in the same way as its parents not its foster-parent. This means the cuckoo must be born with its behavioural instincts as it has no one to learn them from.

Instruments, musical

People have been making music for many years by hitting or blowing through shells, animal horns and other materials. Modern musical instruments can be divided into four groups: woodwind, brass, percussion and strings.

Woodwind instruments such as the recorder make a column of air vibrate inside a tube. The player can change the note produced by covering different holes to change the length of the vibrating air column. Brass

▼ Human babies display a grasping instinct. Some scientists believe that this has been inherited from our tree-dwelling ancestors.

▶ All countries have developed different instruments using material that is available to them. Some of these instruments may make very different sounds to the music we normally hear.

Vibrating skin

▲ When a drum is struck, the vibrations inside the instrument are reflected to and fro. As they lose energy, the sound of the drumbeat gradually dies away.

▼ Some of the sound produced by the vibrating strings is trapped within the violin's delicately shaped body, where it resonates to create a rich tone.

instruments, including the trumpet and trombone, rely on the player blowing through lips tightly pressed against the mouthpiece. This makes a buzzing sound that is expanded and changed by the instrument. Percussion instruments are played by being struck like a drum. The piano is included in the percussion group because it is played by making hammers strike strings. Some stringed instruments such as the violin are played by drawing a bow across the strings to make them vibrate. Others such as the guitar are plucked. Different notes are produced by pressing the strings at different points.

Modern TECHNOLOGY has produced a new type of instrument called a synthesizer. This uses ELECTRONIC circuits to create electrical signals that, when amplified, make a loudspeaker vibrate. Computer controlled synthesizers can imitate other instruments and also make complicated new sounds.

Bow

String

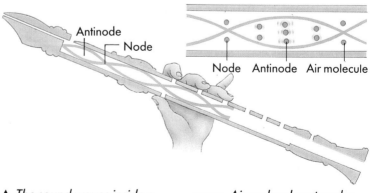

Antinode
Node

Node   Antinode   Air molecule

▲ The sound waves inside a wind instrument, such as a recorder, form a stationary pattern known as a standing wave. Air molecules at nodes do not vibrate, and the distance between nodes determines the pitch of the note.

INSTRUMENTS, SCIENTIFIC ⚙

Scientific instruments are devices, machines and systems used by scientists and engineers for detection, observation, measurement, control, calculation and analysis. Instruments extend the human senses. Some of them detect and measure radiations or particles that are invisible to the human eye. Microscopes and telescopes reveal objects that are too small or too far away to be seen by the unaided eye. Some instruments measure quantities that human senses are incapable of detecting or measuring, such as radio waves. All branches of experimental science depend on instruments.

Scientific instruments are limited by the science and technology of the day. Developments in science may suggest new instruments. For example, electrically powered instruments could not be made until the development of batteries and mains electric power. The electron microscope could not be designed until the structure of the atom and the properties of atomic particles were understood.

Instruments may measure the same property, for example length or distance, in different ways. A micrometer measures the thickness of small objects by clamping the object between two jaws, one of which has a measuring scale engraved on it so the thickness can be read. The distance between the Earth and the Moon was measured most accurately by bouncing a laser beam off a reflector placed on the Moon by the Apollo astronauts. The time taken for the beam to return allowed the distance to be calculated.

All scientific instruments disturb the thing they are measuring and this must be taken into account when instruments are designed. No instrument is absolutely accurate. There are always errors in detection, observation and measurement. The instrument designer must minimize these errors.

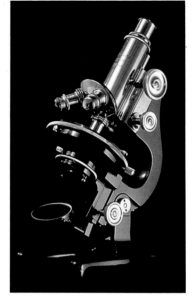

▲ Optical microscopes magnify small objects so that they can be studied in detail. Magnifications of up to 1500 times can be achieved.

▲ Samples of ice and snow brought from the Antarctic contain specks of dust. An instrument called a Coulter counter is used to detect the particles and count them.

◄ Laboratories are equipped with instruments for scientists to do experiments and carry out analysis. These biochemists are analysing samples of tissues for a hospital.

See also ANALYSIS, CHEMICAL; COMPUTER; ELECTRON MICROSCOPE; EXPERIMENT; MEASUREMENT; MICROMETER; MICROSCOPE.

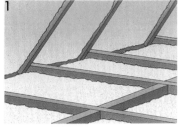

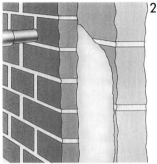

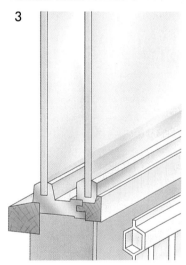

Insulation, thermal

Thermal insulation slows down the flow of HEAT from a hot object to a colder one. Heat can be carried by CONDUCTION, CONVECTION and RADIATION, so thermal insulation must slow down all three. Thermal CONDUCTION can be reduced by using a material in which the electrons are not free to move and carry heat with them (such materials will also be electrical INSULATORS). Convection can be slowed down by limiting the circulation of FLUIDS

> SEE FOR YOURSELF
> Test the thermal insulating properties of different materials by wrapping them around empty drink cans. Then fill the cans with hot water from the same kettle and seal them with modelling clay. Place one unwrapped can of hot water in a sealed glass jar, thus wrapping it in air. Wrap one in newspaper one in thin cotton and one in a thick woolly material. Compare the water temperature in each can after 30 minutes.

which could carry the heat. Radiation can be reduced by using shiny surfaces. A VACUUM prevents conduction and convection, as in a vacuum flask, which keeps hot things hot and cold things cold.

Many mammals and birds are insulated by a layer of fat beneath the SKIN or fur and by FEATHERS which trap a layer of air next to the skin.

▲ Many types of thermal insulation can be added to existing houses in order to reduce heat loss. Glass wool is used to line roof spaces 1, and insulating foam can be pumped into wall cavities 2. Double-glazed windows also lower heat loss 3.

▶ The cockpits of spacecraft are covered with insulation blankets beneath the outer shell. This protects the interior of the craft from the extremes of temperature that may be experienced in outer space.

Insulators, electrical

Electrical insulators are materials which do not conduct ELECTRICITY well. In electrical CONDUCTORS, such as metals, charged particles called ELECTRONS are free to move through the material and carry the electric current; in insulators, however, the electrons are not free to move and cannot carry a current. Materials such as plastics, glass, CERAMICS and rubber are insulators.

Insulators are important because they allow us to confine the flow of electric current to the places where it is wanted; for example, in an ordinary electrical flex, insulation is used to separate the wires which carry current in opposite directions. Insulators are also used to separate the positive and negative charges in a CAPACITOR. A material that is a poor conductor of heat generally is also a poor conductor of electricity.

▲ High-voltage electric cables have to be well insulated. These are heavy duty ceramic insulators.

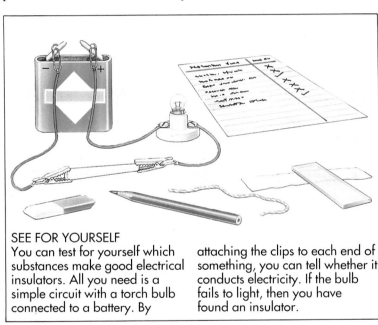

SEE FOR YOURSELF
You can test for yourself which substances make good electrical insulators. All you need is a simple circuit with a torch bulb connected to a battery. By attaching the clips to each end of something, you can tell whether it conducts electricity. If the bulb fails to light, then you have found an insulator.

Integrated circuit

An integrated circuit is an electronic CIRCUIT contained in a paper-thin chip of silicon roughly one centimetre square. The circuit on the chip may contain up to several hundred thousand components. There are different types of circuits on chips. The most important is the MICROPROCESSOR. It forms the calculating and control centre of a COMPUTER. Printed circuit boards may be fitted with sockets into which chips are plugged.

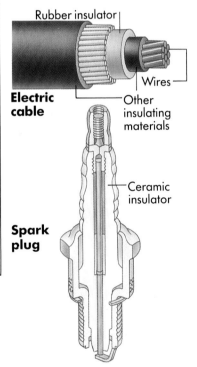

▲ Rubber is the most effective natural electrical insulator, although in modern equipment it has largely been replaced by plastics. Ceramic insulators have many uses, from car spark plugs to power lines.

▶ *The first integrated circuits had fewer than 20 transistors but now, although the circuits are still very small, there may be more than 20,000.*

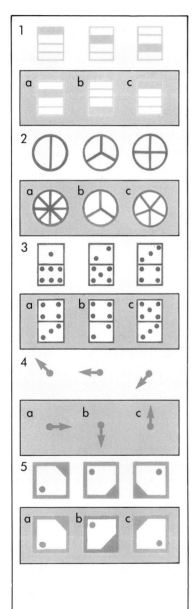

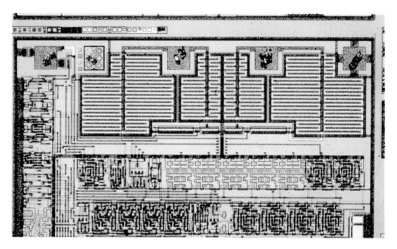

Intelligence

Intelligence has been defined in many different ways, but perhaps the simplest definition is that intelligence is the ability to learn and, when we are talking about people, the ability to understand. All animals can learn to some extent, but some animals are better at it than others. Humans are the most intelligent of all animals.

Psychologists have always been interested in how much of our intelligence is inherited and how much learned. How clever someone is depends on both factors, but whether what you inherit from your CHROMOSOMES AND GENES is more important than what happens to you during your life, is hotly debated. However, there are some people who seem to be born with enormous mental abilities, both in what we call intelligence and talents such as musical or artistic abilities.

Parents and teachers have an important role to play by encouraging children to develop their own mental abilities. If we are not encouraged to read and discuss, to solve problems and to use our intelligence, it will not develop to its full power.

Internal combustion engine

An internal combustion engine is an ENGINE in which the FUEL is burned inside the engine. The engines in modern cars, ships and aircraft are all internal combustion engines. There are three types of internal combustion engines: petrol, DIESEL and GAS TURBINE. In all three, the fuel is burned to heat air. As the air heats up, it expands and this can be made to do useful WORK. In petrol and

SEE FOR YOURSELF
One characteristic of intelligence is the ability to detect patterns. The first 3 pictures in each set follow a pattern. Choose one picture from the second set to complete the patterns. Answers on page 364.

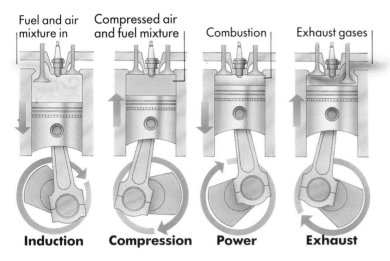

Fuel and air mixture in | Compressed air and fuel mixture | Combustion | Exhaust gases

Induction | **Compression** | **Power** | **Exhaust**

◀ *In a four-stroke car engine, the combustion cycle begins with the induction stroke which pulls a petrol/air mixture into the cylinder. The next stroke compresses the mixture, which is then ignited to produce the power stroke. The exhaust stroke forces waste products out of the cylinder, ready for the next induction stroke.*

diesel engines, the air expands inside a cylinder and pushes against a piston connected to the vehicle's wheels. The petrol engine needs an electrical spark to ignite the fuel but the heavier diesel is ignited by pressure alone. A gas turbine, or jet, engine does not have any cylinders. Air flows through it from front to rear, being compressed by fans and heated on its way through. The engine's thrust is produced by the jet of escaping gases.

The first internal combustion engines built in the 1860s used gas as a fuel. In 1885 Gottlieb Daimler built an internal combustion engine that used a liquid fuel such as petrol. In 1894 another German engineer, Rudolph Diesel, made the first diesel engine. The first practical gas turbines for aircraft were not built until World War II in Britain and Germany. Gas turbines are now often used to power fast boats and military ships. *See also* FLIGHT; JET PROPULSION.

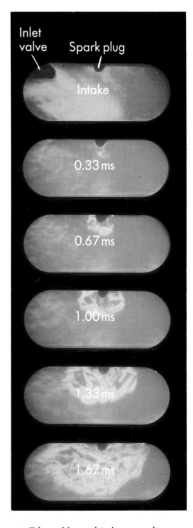

Inlet valve | Spark plug

Intake

0.33 ms

0.67 ms

1.00 ms

1.33 ms

1.67 ms

▲ *Filmed by a high-speed camera, the sequence shows the ignition of the fuel/air mixture inside an engine cylinder. Modern petrols burn very smoothly, reducing engine vibration.*

Nikolaus Otto (1832–1891)
Otto was a German engineer who developed a four-stroke, gas-fuelled internal combustion engine which he patented in 1877. Otto did not invent the four-stroke cycle but was the first to incorporate it into a successful design. Otto's smooth running gas engines were widely used before World War I, after which they were superseded by petrol engines.

▲ As well as the stars and planets in the Universe there are huge clouds of interstellar dust. If you look up to the Milky Way on a clear night you will see a mass of shimmering starlight but also some black areas where there seem to be no stars. This is because great dust clouds are blocking out the starlight behind them.

▶ The process of digestion begins in our mouths. By the time food reaches the small intestine (ileum) it has been broken down into its basic constituents by the action of digestive juices and enzymes. Nearly all the absorption of food takes place in the small intestine. Only water and waste matter pass along to the large intestine.

Interstellar matter

Interstellar means between the STARS, and in our GALAXY this space is occupied by scattered atoms of hydrogen and other ELEMENTS. In some regions these have collected together to form vast dark clouds or NEBULAE.

Some of this matter may be original left-over material from the galaxy's formation. But it is also added to by stars, particularly old RED GIANTS and SUPERNOVAE, pouring material out into space.

See also BIG CRUNCH; MILKY WAY.

Intestine

The intestine is the main part of the digestive system. In humans it consists of a 9m tube stretching from the STOMACH to the anus. Most DIGESTION, the breaking down of food into simple substances which can be absorbed to nourish the body, occurs in the intestine. For its whole length, the intestine is covered with sheets of MUSCLE. These contract in waves to push the partly-digested food along. This process is called *peristalsis*. The intestine is divided into distinct regions according to the ENZYMES produced and the food absorbed at that point. The final parts of the intestine are the wide colon, where the remaining food materials are solidified into faeces, and the short rectum where faeces are stored temporarily until they are discharged from the body.

See also LIVER; PANCREAS.

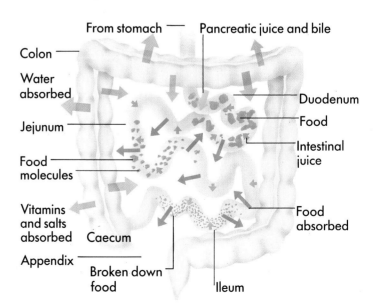

364

Invention

An invention is a new machine, engine, tool or other useful object or process that no one else has thought of before or it can be a major improvement on something someone else has produced. Someone can protect what he or she has invented by applying for a patent. If the authority that grants patents in the inventor's country agrees that the inventor's work is indeed new, a patent is granted. As long as the inventor pays the required fees, the invention cannot be copied or made by anyone else for several years without the inventor's permission. This stops people from stealing an inventor's work. The first known patent for an invention was issued in Florence, Italy, in 1421. Many important inventions have come from the work of one person; others come from many people working as a team.

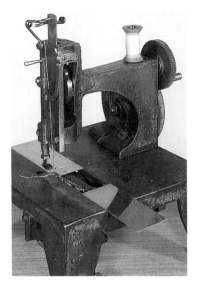

▲ In 1851 Isaac Singer made a considerable improvement to the sewing machine with his invention of the presser foot, which holds the fabric in place while it is being stitched.

Shaduf

◀ The shaduf is an early invention from ancient Egypt, it was used to move water from one place to another. This picture shows it being used in an irrigation system.

Iodine

Iodine is a non-metallic ELEMENT that belongs to the HALOGEN group. At room temperature, iodine is a shiny bluish-black solid with an irritating smell. When heated, it sublimes, that is, it turns directly from a solid into a vapour. Iodine vapour is purple and also possesses an irritating odour. Pure iodine is poisonous if swallowed, but minute amounts of iodine compounds are essential to plants and animals for healthy development. In the human body, the thyroid GLAND in the neck uses iodine to produce a HORMONE vital for healthy physical growth and mental development. Seaweed contains a great deal of iodine. Iodides (iodine SALTS) are used in the photographic industry and in medicine. The RADIOISOTOPE iodine-131 is used for diagnosing and treating diseases related to the thyroid gland.

▲ Iodine and its compounds are used as antiseptics and fungicides and in the manufacture of dyes.

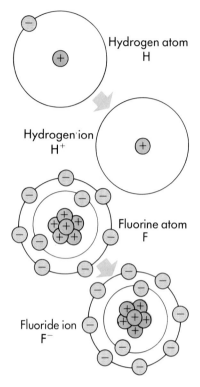

▲ Ions form when atoms and molecules lose or gain an electrical charge. A positive hydrogen ion is formed when a neutrally-charged hydrogen atom loses its negatively charged electron, so that the atom is left with an overall positive charge. A negative fluoride ion is formed when the neutrally-charged atom gains a negatively-charged electron. The additional electron gives the whole atom an overall negative charge.

▶ In an ion motor a power source, such as a nuclear reactor, provides the energy to vaporize caesium. The caesium gas is absorbed by a platinum grid, which re-emits positive ions. Negatively-charged electrons are also given off by the platinum, and the two flows of charged particles are kept separate. Inside the thrust chamber the ions and electrons mix, driving the motor by a jet of neutral atoms.

Ion

An ion is an ATOM or group of atoms that possesses an electric charge through the gain or loss of one or more ELECTRONS. Usually, an atom is neutral (neither positively nor negatively charged) because the number of positively charged protons in its nucleus equals the number of its negatively charged electrons. In certain situations, however, atoms may lose some of their outer electrons to become positively charged ions. This is called ionization. A positive ion is known as a cation. A negatively charged ion is called an anion. Ions of opposite charges attract each other. Common salt (sodium chloride) is a solid crystalline COMPOUND in which positive sodium ions and negative chloride ions are held together by this attraction. During ELECTROLYSIS ions are attracted to electrodes of opposite charges.

Ion propulsion

Ion propulsion is a way of powering a spacecraft. The first ion engines were made at the Lewis Research Center in the United States in the 1960s. They relied on the behaviour of electrically charged particles in an electric field. Negatively charged particles called ELECTRONS were stripped away from mercury or caesium ATOMS, leaving positively charged IONS. When the ions were acted on by an electric field, the forces between the ions and the field made them rush out of the engine through a nozzle, producing thrust.

Ion drives can only accelerate very slowly, but they can last a very long time. They are not used, therefore, for manned flight, but are ideal for long unmanned spaceflights needed for SPACE EXPLORATION.
See also ROCKETS; SPACE PROBES.

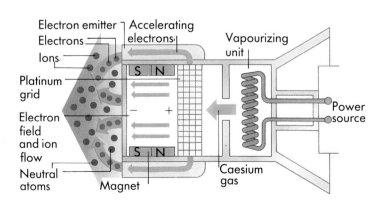

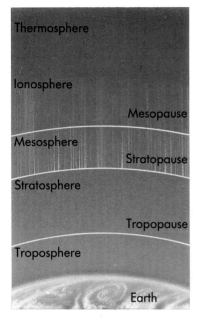

Thermosphere

Ionosphere

Mesopause

Mesosphere

Stratopause

Stratosphere

Tropopause

Troposphere

Earth

◄ *The ionosphere occurs at the upper edge of the atmosphere, about 80 km above the Earth's surface. At these altitudes the air is very thin, and atoms and molecules are easily ionized by high-energy radiation from space. Below the ionosphere, in the troposphere and stratosphere, the air is much denser. Harmful ionizing radiation is absorbed, and virtually none reaches the surface of our planet.*

▶ *In terms of volume, the ionosphere is by far the largest portion of the atmosphere. But the air molecules are so far apart that, in terms of mass, the ionosphere is the smallest part.*

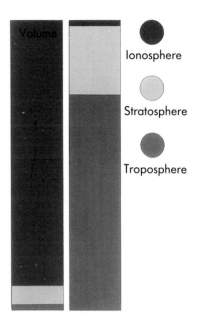

Volume

Ionosphere

Stratosphere

Troposphere

Ionosphere

The ionosphere is the outer region of the Earth's ATMOS-PHERE which lies above a height of 80 km. The ionosphere gets its name because it contains the greatest concentration of IONS.

The ionosphere is vitally important to COMMUNI-CATIONS using RADIO waves. Because the Earth is a sphere and because radio waves can only travel in straight lines, you would expect radio signals would pass straight out into space. But some radio waves are reflected back towards the Earth by the charged particles in the ionosphere, making radio transmissions possible over very long distances around the Earth. Short wave transmissions are reflected more strongly than longer waves, so all long-distance radio communication is carried on short wave bands.

Iridescence

Iridescence is the name given to the multi-coloured rainbow-like reflections which can sometimes be seen from a layer of oil on water, from soap BUBBLES or from certain MINERALS and gems. It happens because LIGHT can bounce back and forth between the top and the bottom of the oil film or between the sides of tiny cracks in the mineral. In some directions, the distance between the sides will be a whole number of WAVELENGTHS of the

Edward Appleton (1892–1965)
Appleton was the British physicist who discovered one of the layers of ionized particles that reflect radio waves in the ionosphere. This layer was often known as the Appleton layer, but is now understood to be two separate layers that are known as F1 and F2. Appleton's work in atmospheric physics was important to the development of radar, and in 1947 he was awarded the Nobel Prize for Physics.

▶ *The beautiful colours in the tail feathers of a peacock are produced by iridescence.*

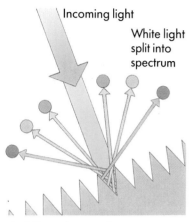

Incoming light

White light split into spectrum

▲ *Minerals sometimes appear iridescent because the light striking them is reflected to and fro between tiny irregularities on the surface. Iridescence on oily water is caused by light refracting through thin films of oil of differing thickness.*

ELECTROMAGNETIC RADIATION which makes up the light, so the peaks and the troughs of the waves which have travelled back and forth once, twice and so on will reinforce each other. Different COLOURS have different wavelengths, so the direction in which the light has to be travelling for this to happen is different for each colour, so you see different colours which change all the time.

Henry Bessemer (1813–1898)
Bessemer was a British steel manufacturer who invented a cheap method for making large quantities of steel. At the heart of the process was the Bessemer converter, a large pear-shaped blast furnace. In the United States, Henry Kelly independently devised a similar process.

Iron and Steel

Iron is a metallic ELEMENT which in its pure form is silvery-white in appearance. Our main sources of iron are ORES such as hematite and magnetite, in which the metal is combined with oxygen to form compounds. Iron is naturally magnetic and combines easily with non-metals such as oxygen. Rust is iron oxide.

Pure iron can be cheaply extracted from ore in a BLAST FURNACE. The ore is heated with coke (carbon) and limestone to produce impure iron called pig iron. Pig iron is purified by being returned to a furnace along with scrap iron and more limestone to produce pure iron. Wrought iron is a type of iron which can be hammered into different shapes and drawn out into thin wires. Most iron goes into making different types of steel. The iron is mixed with carbon, and sometimes other elements to give it extra HARDNESS. Ordinary steel contains up to 1.7 percent carbon. It is used for building ships, bridges and car bodies and rusts easily so needs to be coated with paint or plastic, or with a protective layer such as zinc. The

◄ *Electric arc furnaces for making steel use graphite electrodes to conduct electricity to the contents and generate intense heat.*

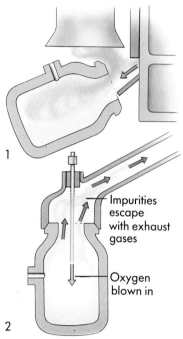

1

2

Impurities escape with exhaust gases

Oxygen blown in

3

Molten steel

Ingot

steel often used for cutlery and saucepans is a more expensive, non-rusting STAINLESS STEEL.

Iron is essential to CELLS in the human body, especially red BLOOD cells. Too little iron in the diet can cause conditions such as anemia.

Irradiation

Irradiation is the exposing of something to RADIATION. This could be in the form of either ELECTROMAGNETIC RADIATION such as ultraviolet light, X-rays or gamma rays, or particles from radioactive materials. Radiation above a certain level is harmful to organisms and it can be used to kill MICROORGANISMS. In FOOD PRESERVATION, irradiation is sometimes used to kill the microorganisms that could spoil or rot food. X-rays and some radioactive particles are used in medicine and industry. The internal structure of a human being can be seen by irradiating the body from one side and placing a radiation detector on

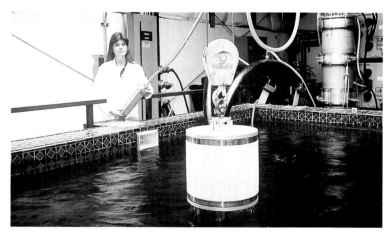

▲ *The basic oxygen process produces steel in a pear-shaped vessel that rests on pivots. The vessel is tilted for loading with scrap iron 1, but returns to the upright position while oxygen is blown in 2. After refining, the vessel is tilted again to pour off the molten steel 3.*

◄ *Fruit is lowered under water before being exposed to X-rays. Irradiation prolongs the life of perishable foods.*

369

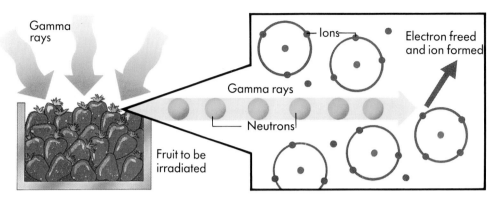

▲ Gamma rays resemble very high-energy X-rays. They can be used to irradiate food, such as fruit. This kills the germs and organisms that make food go bad. For this reason irradiated food keeps fresh for a long time.

the other side. The amount of radiation used must be controlled carefully to prevent destruction of cells.

Irrigation

Irrigation describes the ways in which WATER is brought to land that is too dry for growing plants. Methods of irrigation have been used for over 5000 years.

Irrigation plays an important part in AGRICULTURE today. Farmers can use land normally too dry for farming. The pumps of modern irrigation systems can move millions of litres of water a day. Some systems take water from underground wells, but most systems get water from rivers that have been dammed. Pumps force water from the dam into canals or concrete channels. Pumping stations keep the water moving over long distances. These canals branch into smaller canals across the fields. Sometimes a whole field is flooded at regular intervals. Rows of sprinklers may be placed in a field. Irrigation has disadvantages too. Land can become so waterlogged that plant roots rot and die. Irrigation water may contain SALTS which can poison the plants.

▲ Movable sprinklers are a versatile method of irrigation. They can be moved to irrigate different areas and the amount of water can be controlled.

▶ Irrigation projects and hydroelectric power stations may both make use of water from a reservoir. Irrigation schemes often pump water into secondary canals for distribution at right angles to the flow of the main river.

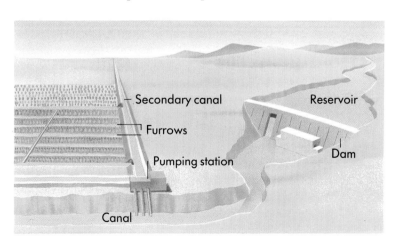

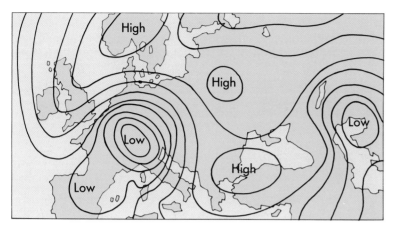

◄ *Weather maps use isobars to show atmospheric pressure. Because the different pressure systems cause different types of weather, such maps can be used to predict the weather. A high-pressure system, such as the one over central Europe, is also known as an anti-cyclone. Anti-cyclones usually bring clear skies and fine weather.*

Isobar

The word 'isobar' comes from a Greek word, *isobares*, which means 'equal weight'. An isobar is a line drawn on a weather chart joining up points of equal atmospheric PRESSURE. Isobars are similar to contours on an ordinary map which join up points of equal altitude.

The closer the isobars are together, the steeper the gradient of pressure difference over a given distance. Air moves from an area of high pressure to an area of low pressure, and the greater the pressure gradient, the faster the flow of air will be and the stronger the wind.

Isomer

An isomer is one of two or more COMPOUNDS in which the same atoms are present in the same proportions but in different arrangements. For example, butane and methylpropane are isomers. They both consist of carbon and hydrogen atoms and both have the formula C_4H_{10}.

Iso at the beginning of a word means equal or identical.
Isobar is a line on a weather map joining places of equal atmospheric pressure.
Isometric objects have equal dimensions or measurements.
Isosceles triangles have two sides of equal length.
Isotonic fluids are fluids with equal osmotic pressure.
Isotopes are atoms with the same atomic number but a different number of neutrons.

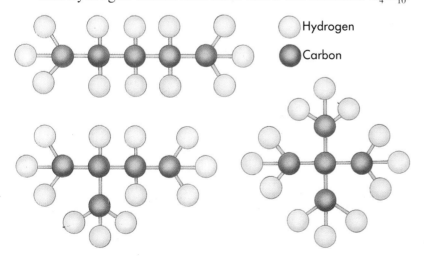

○ Hydrogen
● Carbon

◄ *Pentane has three possible isomers based on different arrangements of the five carbon atoms and twelve hydrogen atoms – a straight chain, a branched chain and a symmetrical cross. The different isomers have different chemical and physical properties.*

371

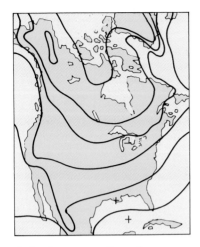

▲ Isotherms are lines drawn on a map joining places which have the same average temperature. The map shows the January isotherms in North America. The cooling influence of the cold arctic seawater filling Canada's Hudson Bay is visible by the way the −30°C isotherm dips sharply southwards. The long mountain chains down the western and eastern coasts of Mexico have a similar effect. These mountains isolate central Mexico from the effect of the much warmer oceans.

But in butane, the four carbon atoms are linked together in a straight chain, while in methylpropane, the carbon atoms form a branched chain with only three carbon atoms in the chain. Isomers may differ in their physical characteristics. The two forms of butane are colourless gases but methylpropane has a lower boiling point (−12°C) than butane (−0.5°C).

Isotherm

An isotherm is a line drawn on a CLIMATE chart joining points on the Earth that have the same TEMPERATURE at a particular time or where the temperature, averaged throughout the year, is the same.

Isotherms usually record the temperature as though it had been measured at sea level but, obviously, not all weather stations can be at zero height above sea level. To allow for the effects of PRESSURE resulting from the height of the station, the temperatures are adjusted by adding 1°C for each 165 m above sea level.

Isotonic

Two FLUIDS are said to be isotonic when they have the same osmotic pressure. Osmotic pressure is the PRESSURE which builds up in an enclosed space, such as a CELL, when a fluid enters the cell through the cell's semipermeable membrane. Fluid will pass through the membrane until the osmotic pressure is the same as on the other side. When this moment is reached, the fluids are said to be isotonic.

▶ Many of the fluids in the bodies of living organisms consist of a solution of sugar (glucose) in water. The membrane surrounding a cell permits small molecules such as water to pass through it, but not those of glucose. The cell remains isotonic by adjusting its internal osmotic pressure to that of the surrounding fluid, by gaining or losing water molecules.

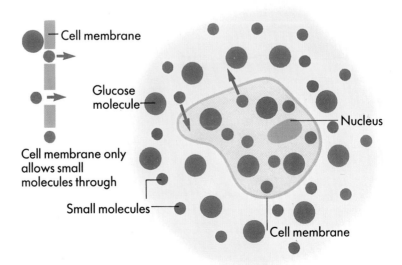

Cell membrane

Glucose molecule

Nucleus

Cell membrane only allows small molecules through

Small molecules

Cell membrane

The movement of fluids in and out of cells is essential to the life of an organism. Most solids and gases travel around in solutions and it is in this way that food matter is passed into cells and waste matter and harmful material pass out.

See also HYPERTONIC; HYPOTONIC; OSMOSIS.

Isotope

An isotope is one of two or more ATOMS of the same ELEMENT that differ from each other in ATOMIC WEIGHT. Isotopes of an element will all have the same number of protons in each of their nuclei but a different number of neutrons. A few elements, such as fluorine, gold and manganese, have no isotopes, but most do. Different isotopes of an element are frequently found together in the same sample. For instance, in any sample of chlorine, 76 percent of the atoms have 18 neutrons and 24 percent have atoms with 20 neutrons. Many elements have a group of isotopes that are stable, but other elements have one or more radioactive isotopes, RADIOISOTOPES. Radioisotopes have a regular rate of decay (HALF-LIFE) that we can use as a kind of clock. For example, carbon-14 is used in this way. Radioisotopes of iodine and cobalt are used in medicine.

Frederick Soddy (1877–1956)
Soddy was a British chemist who worked alongside Ernest Rutherford and carried out pioneering research into radioactive decay. As a result, Soddy was able to formulate the theory of isotopes, and in 1921 he was awarded the Nobel Prize for Chemistry. Aware of the great potential of the energy contained in uranium, he became increasingly concerned about the use of atomic energy and the social responsibility of scientists.

◀ *This piece of equipment contains a radioisotope which is being used to test pipelines under the sea for faults.*

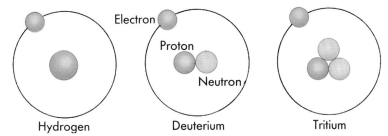

Hydrogen   Deuterium   Tritium

◀ *Hydrogen has three isotopes. Protium, which has a nucleus of one proton, makes up nearly all naturally-occurring hydrogen. The isotope deuterium has a nucleus of one proton and one neutron. The third isotope, tritium, has a nucleus of one proton and two neutrons.*

Frank Whittle (1907–1996)
Whittle, an officer in the British Royal Air Force, built the first successful jet engine in the 1940s. Whittle's turbojet design powered the world's first practical jet aircraft, the Gloster *Meteor*, the prototype of which first flew in 1941. The first jet-engined aircraft actually to fly was the German Heinkel He-178 in 1939. But this later proved impractical.

▶ *Jet propulsion is essential to attain high speeds, and at high altitudes a jet engine is more efficient than a propeller.*

▶ *Squid developed the principle of jet propulsion hundreds of millions of years ago, but can only travel backwards. Squid draw water into their body cavity, then contract powerful muscles that force the water out through forward-pointing nozzles.*

Jenner, Edward *See Vaccination*

Jet propulsion

Jet propulsion is a way of powering something, usually an aircraft, by the force of a fast-moving stream of hot gas, using an ENGINE called a GAS TURBINE invented by Frank Whittle. Air is sucked into the front of the engine by a large spinning fan. Inside the engine, another fan compresses the air and pushes it into a COMBUSTION chamber, or burning chamber. Here, FUEL is sprayed into the air and burned. As the burning mixture of fuel and air heats up it expands and forces its way through the driven (rear) fan and out through the tail-pipe. The rear fan is connected to and turns the compressor. This is the basic gas turbine or jet engine.

There are other types of gas turbine. In a turbofan engine, the jet of hot gas rotates a fan that pushes a large mass of air past the engine. In a turboprop engine, the jet spins a turbine connected to a propeller. A turboshaft engine uses the jet to rotate a turbine connected to a shaft which in turn rotates a helicopter's rotor blades.
See also INTERNAL COMBUSTION ENGINE.

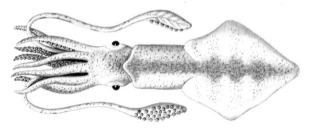

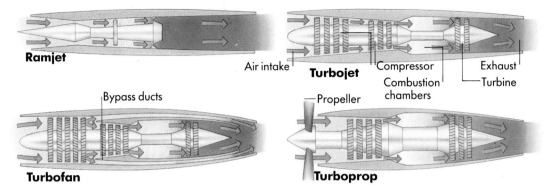

Ramjet

Air intake **Turbojet** Compressor Exhaust

Combustion Turbine
chambers

Bypass ducts Propeller

Turbofan **Turboprop**

Jet stream

In METEOROLOGY, a jet stream is a horizontal band of air which blows as an icy-cold and high-speed wind at heights of between about 10 and 15 km. Sometimes jet stream winds may reach speeds of more than 300 km/h.

The polar jet stream occurs in middle to high LATITUDES where polar and tropical air masses meet. The subtropical jet stream occurs in the regions between the tropics and temperate areas of the world. Unlike the polar and subtropical jet streams, the equatorial jet stream occurs only over south east Asia and Africa, and only in the summer.

▲ *The ramjet is the simplest jet engine. It has neither compressor nor turbine, and is used in missiles. The turbojet is the most common type of engine on commercial airliners; the turbofan engine is a more fuel-efficient alternative. The turboprop gains most of its thrust from the propeller.*

▼ *The polar and subtropical jet streams weaken during the summer and move further north.*

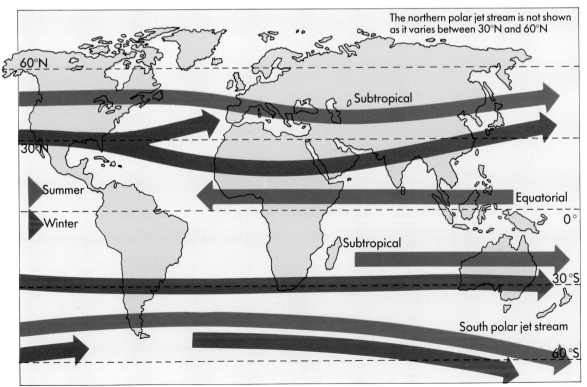

The northern polar jet stream is not shown as it varies between 30°N and 60°N

60°N

Subtropical

30°N

Summer

Equatorial

Winter

0°

Subtropical

30°S

South polar jet stream

60°S

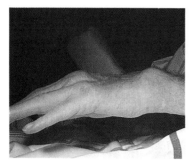

▲ *The deformed hands of someone suffering from severe arthritis. Joints in the hands are among those most frequently affected by crippling arthritis.*

▼ *The most useful joint in the human body is the one that places our thumb opposite our fingers. The opposable thumb makes the human hand one of the most sophisticated natural devices, capable of a wide range of holding and turning movements. No other animal can match human dexterity.*

Joints

Joints are the points at which parts of something meet. In a human body, some joints, like those between most of the BONES of the skull, are rigidly fixed, but the most important joints have a complicated structure to allow them to move freely. The bones are joined by flexible strands of ligament, which stop the joint from popping apart. The ends of the bones are capped with rubbery cartilage, which cushions the shocks caused by walking and other movements, and also provides a slippery bearing surface. The most important joints have a flexible bag between the ends of the bones, containing synovial fluid. This acts like oil, to allow the joint to move without any FRICTION. In arthritis, this synovial joint becomes inflamed and damaged so the joint wears itself away, sometimes right down to the bone.

The structure of a joint also varies according to the type of movement it must make. For example, the knees and elbows work with a simple hinge-like action, and their joints cannot move in any other way. The shoulder and hip, however, must allow limb movement in any direction, so they are ball and socket joints. The joints between vertebrae in the spine allow only a small amount of movement, while keeping the whole structure of the spine very strong.

See also SKELETON.

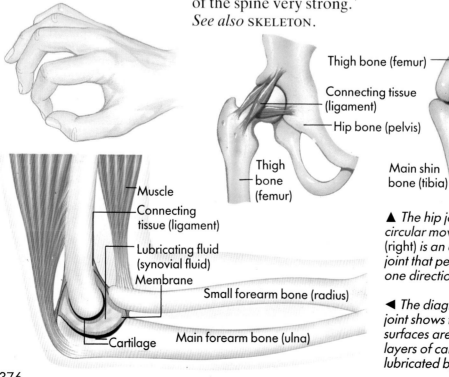

Thigh bone (femur)

Connecting tissue (ligament)

Hip bone (pelvis)

Thigh bone (femur)

Connecting tissue (ligament)

Small shin bone (fibula)

Main shin bone (tibia)

▲ *The hip joint* (left) *permits circular movement; the knee* (right) *is an example of a hinge joint that permits movement in one direction only.*

Muscle

Connecting tissue (ligament)

Lubricating fluid (synovial fluid)

Membrane

Small forearm bone (radius)

Main forearm bone (ulna)

Cartilage

◄ *The diagram of the elbow joint shows that the moving surfaces are protected by layers of cartilage, and lubricated by synovial fluid.*

Joule

The joule (J) is the SI UNIT of ENERGY. The joule is named after a British scientist, James Prescott Joule who was born in Salford in 1818. Although there are many different types of energy, the joule is defined to be equal to the WORK which is done when a FORCE of one newton moves through a distance of one metre in the direction of the force. So, for example, if you need a force of one newton from your hand to lift up an apple and you move it up through a distance of one metre, you have used one joule of energy.

The kilojoule (kJ) is equal to one thousand joules. One joule per second is called a WATT. To boil a kettle containing a litre of water takes about 340,000 J; this amount of energy would also keep a 60 W electric light bulb alight for an hour and a half. The kinetic energy of a one tonne car travelling at 100 km/h is about 400,000 J.

Energy used to be measured in calories (1 calorie equals 4.2 J). The energy values of various different foods are given in joules, kilojoules and kilocalories.

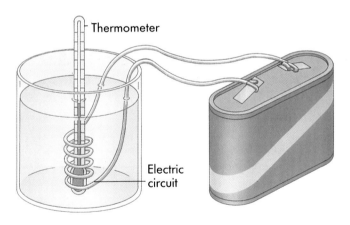

Thermometer

Electric circuit

Joule's law

Joule's law states how much HEAT is generated when an electric current is passed through an electrical CONDUCTOR. Joule found that when mechanical ENERGY was converted to electrical energy, the amount of heat produced was always in proportion to the energy converted. So, the amount of heat that develops in a wire carrying a current is proportional to the resistance of the wire and the square of the current. If one wants to reduce the production of heat, for example in power lines, it is necessary to keep the current flowing as small as possible.

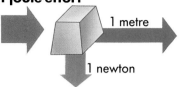

1 joule effort

1 metre

1 newton

▲ *In SI units, one joule of work is done when a force of one newton moves through a distance of one metre.*

James Joule (1818–1889)
James Prescott Joule was a British physicist who studied with Lord Kelvin and the chemist John Dalton. His experiments showed that the production of heat is always accompanied by a loss of another form of energy and so he deduced that heat itself is a form of energy. The unit of energy is named after him.

◀ *A simple experiment to demonstrate Joule's law. Heat produced by the electric current causes the water temperature to rise steadily. The wire is electrically insulated but still able to pass heat to the water.*

Jupiter Facts
Diameter at the equator
142,800 km
Diameter at the poles
134,000 km
Distance from Sun
816,000,000 km (maximum)
741,000,000 km (minimum)
Length of year 11.9 y
Length of day 9h 50 min
Mass 318 Earths
Density 0.39 Earth
Surface Temperature −150°C

▶ *Turbulent winds and storms above the planet's surface create dramatic patterns in Jupiter's cloud layer.*

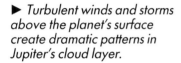

▲ *Jupiter has a diameter of 134,200 km at the poles, and has a mass 318 times that of Earth.*

▼ *The moons orbiting Jupiter include the Galilean satellites, Io, Europa, Ganymede and Callisto.*

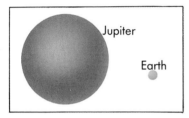

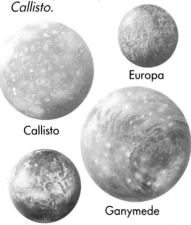

Callisto

Europa

Ganymede

Io

Jupiter

Jupiter is the largest PLANET in the SOLAR SYSTEM. It is so huge that a thousand Earths could fit inside it, but it spins so fast its 'day' is less than 10 hours long. This rapid whirling has made its equator bulge outwards.

Like the other giant planets (SATURN, URANUS and NEPTUNE), Jupiter is made up mostly of hydrogen. Bands and whirls of other frozen chemicals, such as water and ammonia, howl through the cloudy surface at hurricane force. The famous Great Red Spot is the top of a long lasting cyclone or whirlwind larger than the Earth. But although the temperature of these top layers is about −150°C, the centre of the planet is believed to be hotter than the surface of the Sun.

Jupiter and the other giant planets are made up of gas rather than rock and metal because they are so large. Molecules of gases fly about faster than molecules of solids and need stronger GRAVITY to hold them down. Small planets like Earth cannot hold on to hydrogen.

Jupiter has 18 known satellites. Four of them are at least as large as our own MOON and they are visible with good binoculars. Voyagers 1 and 2 have shown that Callisto and Ganymede are covered with Moon-like craters, Europa is a smooth ball of ice, and Io, nearest to Jupiter, has a yellow sulphur-covered surface and volcanoes erupting material 100 km into space.

Kaleidoscope

A kaleidoscope is an instrument or toy containing MIR-RORS which make multiple reflections and so create random regular patterns. It consists of a tube, usually about 30 cm long, with two or three long thin mirrors running the length of the tube. The mirrors are fixed in the tube at an angle to each other, usually 60 degrees.

The most common kaleidoscope has one end of the tube covered by a piece of ground glass or a similar semi-transparent plastic sheet. The other end of the tube has a small peep-hole in it. The tube also contains small pieces of coloured glass or plastic. When the tube is held up to the eye and turned, the coloured pieces tumble around the far end of the tube randomly. Several images of each piece are seen because they are reflected in the mirrors.

SEE FOR YOURSELF

To make your own kaleidoscope, tape together 3 mirrors of the same size as shown in the illustration. Tape a triangular piece of tracing paper to one end. Put some coloured pieces of paper, cut into interesting shapes, inside the tube you have just made. Hold the kaleidoscope upright and look down inside to see the beautiful pattern made by the reflections. To change the pattern simply shake the kaleidoscope to move the pieces of paper.

▼ *William Thomson, Lord Kelvin was an energetic and enthusiastic scientist and worked with many leading scientists of his day. He worked with Joule on the relation between heat and work.*

▶ *On the absolute temperature scale, temperatures are given in kelvins (K). An object's temperature is a measure of its energy. At 0 K, called absolute zero, an object has no energy at all. The word 'degree' and its symbol (°) are not used with kelvins.*

▲ *Kepler mainly studied the planets but also carried out important research into optics.*

Kelvin (K)

The kelvin is the unit used to measure the absolute TEMPERATURE of a system. Whereas the zero of the CELSIUS temperature scale happens to be chosen as the freezing point of a common substance (water), at zero kelvin an object is as cold as it can be. No further heat can be taken from it. Zero kelvin is –273.15°C. One kelvin is equivalent to one degree on the Celsius scale. It may be impossible to reach absolute zero, but scientists have cooled systems to a few millionths of a degree above absolute zero.

Kelvin, William Thomson

William Thomson (1824–1907), later Lord Kelvin of Largs, was a British physicist and engineer who was born in Belfast and died near Largs, Scotland. He entered the University of Glasgow when he was 10, published his first scientific article at 16 and went on to study at Cambridge. In 1846 he became a professor in Glasgow. He was one of the first people to state the Second Law of THERMODYNAMICS that HEAT cannot be completely converted into WORK. He also estimated the age of the Earth

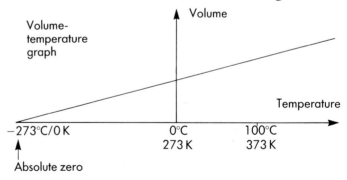

Volume-temperature graph

Volume

Temperature

−273°C/0 K   0°C   100°C
273 K   373 K

↑ Absolute zero

from its temperature, although he was wrong because he did not know about the production of heat through RADIOACTIVITY in the Earth. He became rich because of his design for a GALVANOMETER to receive the signals sent through underwater TELEGRAPH cables.

Kepler, Johannes

Kepler (1571–1630) proved that the EARTH and the other PLANETS in the SOLAR SYSTEM orbit the SUN in elliptical paths. Kepler was born in what is now southwestern Germany. He was very frail, and often ill but a brilliant

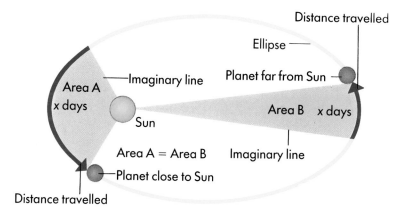

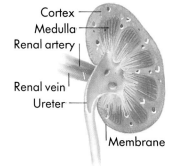

◄ Kepler's second law of planetary motion states that an imaginary line between the Sun and a planet always sweeps through the same area during the same time. Planets therefore travel fastest when nearest the Sun.

▲ *Cross-section of a kidney.*

▼ *Magnified detail of an individual filtration tubule, showing the area where urine is separated from the blood.*

mathematician. He worked with Tycho BRAHE in Prague and built on his theories and those of COPERNICUS. Copernicus was the first to show that the Earth revolved around the Sun. After years of painstaking observations and calculation Kepler discovered planets do not move in circles as Copernicus believed, but ellipses, which are like flattened circles.

Finally he published his laws of planetary motion to explain the motion of the planets. Kepler also believed in astrology and earned money casting horoscopes.

Kerosene *See* Paraffin

Kidneys

Kidneys, in humans, are paired organs at the back of the abdomen, on either side of the spine. They remove waste products from the BLOOD, passing them out of the body as urine. They do this by filtering the blood. Each kidney contains millions of tiny tubular filtration devices, called nephrons. Blood enters the kidney in small capillaries, and passes through a tiny knot of blood vessels sitting at the top of the nephron. Water and dissolved materials pass through the wall of the blood vessel into the nephron, and are carried down into the kidney along a twisted tube. As it passes along this tube, most of the water and many dissolved useful substances are absorbed back into the blood again, leaving concentrated urine, containing urea, in the tube. This waste material is produced as the body uses protein, and since it is poisonous, it is important that it is removed efficiently. If the kidneys fail, dialysis must be used to remove wastes from the blood, by filtering it in a machine or the patient must have a kidney TRANSPLANT.

Kidney tubule (Nephron)

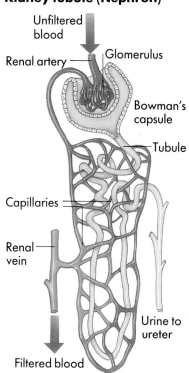

▶ This kiln in Bahrain is typical of those used there for firing pottery or for roasting limestone to make lime.

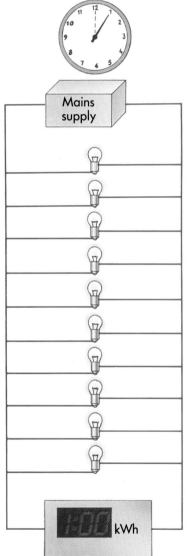

▲ Ten 100-watt light bulbs (1000 watts in total – a kilowatt) burning for one hour use one kilowatt-hour (or unit) of electrical energy.

382

Kiln

A kiln is an oven or furnace used for drying and hardening objects made from clay such as bricks, plates and cups. The process, called firing, was done in ancient times by placing the object in an open fire. The kiln allows things to be heated to much higher temperatures. Fires burning underneath the kiln heated air which flowed through the kiln, heating the objects inside. Kilns range in size from small table-top models used to fire one or two pots to commercial kilns with space for thousands of bricks. Modern kilns are heated by gas or electricity.

Kilowatt-hour

The kilowatt-hour (kWh) is a measure of electrical ENERGY. It is the energy used when an electrical appliance with a POWER of one kilowatt is run for one hour. Since a power of one watt corresponds to using one JOULE of energy every second, a kilowatt-hour corresponds to 3,600,000 J. One bar of an electric fire uses about 1 kW of electrical energy, so it uses up one kilowatt-hour of energy every hour.

Kinetic energy *See* Energy

Koch, Robert *See* Medicine

Laboratory

When we think of a laboratory, we usually imagine a special room where scientific equipment is kept and EXPERIMENTS are carried out. Laboratory experiments are carried out under conditions where all the factors that might affect the outcome of the experiment are strictly controlled. There are different types of laboratories, their design and the things in them depend on the kinds of experiments that are to be done in them. All laboratories have some scientific INSTRUMENTS in them. The school laboratory has BUNSEN BURNERS and maybe a CENTRIFUGE. Laboratories often contain dangerous chemicals and equipment, even school laboratories. New products are developed and tested in laboratories. Many famous discoveries, such as the discovery of RADIUM, have been made in laboratories. New products and medicines have to go through many tests in laboratories before people can buy them.

People can also be studied in a laboratory. An experimenter may wish to find out, for example, how people perform in a memory test taken on their own or with a

Laboratory Safety
Scientists always observe safe practices to make sure accidents do not happen.
● Keep chemicals in safe containers.
● Wash your hands before and afterwards.
● Never put chemicals near your face or mess about with them to see what happens.

SEE FOR YOURSELF
Simple experiments can be done at home and you can make your own laboratory equipment using everyday objects. A filter funnel can be made from the top part of a plastic bottle and coffee filter papers can be placed inside it. A clothes peg firmly attached to a wooden handle is good for holding hot test tubes. Things can be heated safely by placing them in very hot water in a heat-proof jug. You can heat substances more strongly with a nightlight placed in sand in a metal tray, rest a cooking rack on 2 bricks above the flame and things can be heated in heat-proof dishes. A test tube rack can be made from a shoe box. An eye dropper will measure accurate amounts of liquid. Modelling clay can be used to seal all kinds of things.

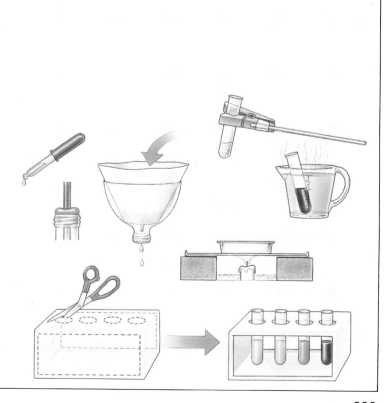

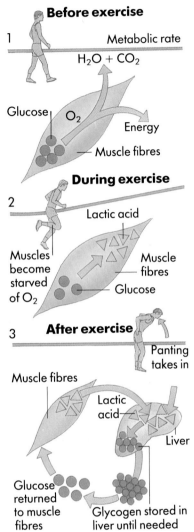

Before exercise

1

Metabolic rate

$H_2O + CO_2$

Glucose | O_2

Energy

Muscle fibres

During exercise

2

Lactic acid

Muscles become starved of O_2

Muscle fibres

Glucose

3

After exercise

Panting takes in

Muscle fibres

Lactic acid

Liver

Glucose returned to muscle fibres

Glycogen stored in liver until needed

▶ *Laboratory instruments help in the search for oil.*

◀ *During gentle exercise, glucose in muscles is used up to provide energy producing carbon dioxide and water as well 1. In vigorous exercise there may not be enough oxygen to break down the glucose, so the glucose is converted into lactic acid 2. When there is plenty of oxygen in the blood again, the lactic acid is converted into glycogen and then glucose 3.*

group, at different times of day or in noise or quiet. These conditions can be controlled in a laboratory.

Lactic acid

Lactic acid is a colourless or yellowish liquid. It is commonly found in sour MILK or other dairy products that have curdled. It is also found in pickles and beer and is formed by the FERMENTATION of sugar. Lactic acid is produced commercially by fermentation and is used in the tanning and textile industries and to flavour food.

Lactic acid is often present in the BLOOD of people and animals. Normally when our MUSCLES need energy it is produced by the breakdown of CARBOHYDRATES by OXYGEN. However, in strenuous exercise the blood cannot deliver oxygen fast enough and so carbohydrate is broken down anaerobically (without oxygen). This produces lactic acid which can give a characteristic pain in muscle, called a 'stitch'.

Lamarck, Jean Baptiste

Jean Baptiste Lamarck (1744–1829) was a French biologist, best known for his attempts to explain EVOLUTION. He suggested that useful features acquired during the life of an individual could pass to the next generation, thus making each generation more efficient. Lamarck believed that giraffes stretched their necks as they reached for leaves, and then passed their longer necks on to their offspring. According to his theory, a person who trained to become an athlete would have athletic children. Neither Lamarck nor anyone else could

▲ *Lamarck was one of the first to propose a theory of evolution.*

384

First generation

Second generation

Third generation

provide any evidence for this kind of evolution and few people believed his theory. Body CELLS and reproductive cells are quite separate, and only the genes in the reproductive cells are passed on to the offspring.
See also CHROMOSOMES AND GENES; NATURAL SELECTION.

▲ *Lamarck's idea that animals 'improved' themselves through generations of effort, made for an attractive theory of evolution. But he was fundamentally mistaken; animals cannot rewrite their own genetic codes. Darwin's theory of evolution showed that animals do adapt to their environment, but that changes occur as a result of random mutation, modified by the process of natural selection.*

Laminates

Laminates are MATERIALS made by gluing thin layers of material together, usually under PRESSURE. The result is a strong yet thin sheet. Laminating materials can increase their strength. A thin sheet of wood resists bending along the grain of the wood, but it bends easily and breaks across the grain. If several sheets of wood are glued together so that the grain of each sheet lies in a different direction, the weakness of one sheet is offset by the strength of the next. The result, called plywood, is a very strong building material.

Plastics and new materials such as CARBON FIBRE are also often laminated for the same reasons. Some materials are sealed inside a more attractive and hard-wearing laminate such as a thin layer of plastic material. Many kitchen surfaces are made of chipboard laminates.

▲ *This wood has been laminated with a special metal surface.*

Landforms

Landform is the form, or shape, of the surface of the EARTH's land masses. In other words, landforms are the relief (the hills and valleys) of the land. The science, a branch of GEOGRAPHY, which studies landforms is called geomorphology. *See* pages 386 and 387.

LANDFORMS

Landforms are mostly shaped by the rocks which lie beneath the land, by their type and structure. For example, an old, hard, metamorphic rock is likely to be more resistant to the effects of erosion and weathering than a younger, soft clay is. Consequently, such hard rocks may give rise to upstanding hills or mountains while the clay may underlie a valley floor or a flat plain. Similarly, a block of rock which has been 'faulted' downwards may produce a valley while rocks that have been 'folded' may become a mountain chain.

Another important condition which affects landforms is climate which, together with the rocks, governs the soil type of the area and affects the plant life that grows there. These three linked conditions play a major part in forming the foundations of the land. For example, a landscape which is subjected to the dry heating and cooling of desert conditions where there is little or no soil and only sparse plant life will be quite different to that of a tropical rainforest or to one which has been affected by glaciers.

The final condition determining landforms is the age of the landscape, the length of time to which the land has been subjected to weathering and erosion. For example, a mountain chain newly thrust up by the movements of the Earth's crust will have a different appearance to old mountain scenery where rivers and glaciers, freezing and thawing have shaped the rocks over millions of years.

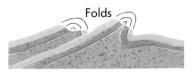

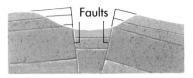

▲ *The original folds and faults in the Earth's surface have undergone centuries of erosion to become the landforms that we see today.*

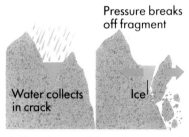

▲ *Frost is one of the main causes of weathering in rocks. Rainwater seeps into cracks, then expands with great force when it freezes, breaking the rock into pieces.*

◄ *Two prominent buttes stick up above the surrounding desert in Monument Valley, Arizona, United States.*

▼ *Simple folding produces hills and valleys (anticlines and synclines). When a fold collapses onto itself it forms a nappe. The complexity of the folding is hidden underground.*

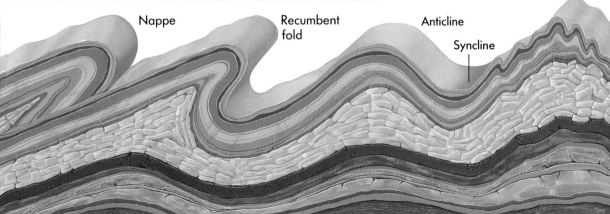

Nappe   Recumbent fold   Anticline   Syncline

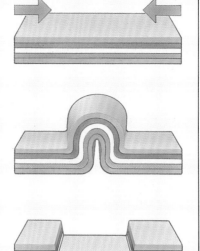

▲ Formed when the land shifted in prehistoric times, the Great Rift Valley runs through eastern Africa. It is mostly about 40 km wide and in some places is over 1 km deep.

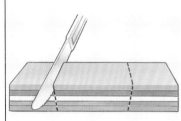

▶ The badlands in South Dakota, United States, have been made into a national park. Badlands are formed mainly by water erosion. Flashfloods cause the most erosion, wearing away great areas.

▼ Faults occur when rock strata are shifted up or down by movements in the Earth's crust. An uplifted mass of rock may form a block mountain (or horst). The steep side is often called an escarpment. A valley created by a descending mass of rock is known as a rift valley. Both landforms have distinctive flat and level surfaces.

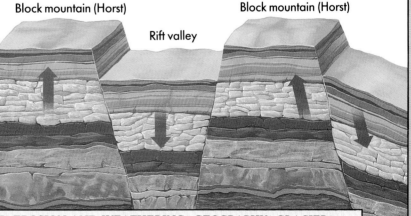

Valley

Fault

Block mountain (Horst)

Rift valley

Block mountain (Horst)

See also DESERT; EARTH; EROSION AND WEATHERING; GEOGRAPHY; GLACIER; MOUNTAINS; RIVERS AND LAKES; ROCKS; SOIL.

▲ *A tiny microcomputer is at the heart of this portable language translator, used by businessmen and holidaymakers abroad.*

The principal purpose of larvae is to eat, and for many insects the larval diet is completely different from the insect's adult diet. It is thought that this is very advantageous because the larvae and the adults do not compete for the same food.

Language translation by computers

Language translation by computers is the conversion of one language into another by a COMPUTER. Words in one language and their equivalent words in another language can be stored in a COMPUTER MEMORY. If the computer is given a word, it produces the equivalent word in the other language. To translate sentences is more complicated than translating a single word because the rules for putting words together are different in different languages. However, there are computer programs which include these rules and can translate sentences.

Larva

This name is given to the young form of an animal when it is distinctly different from the adult stage. The best known larvae are caterpillars, which eventually grow up into butterflies and moths. Other insects with larvae include flies, many of whose larvae are called maggots, and beetles. Not all insects have larvae. Young grasshoppers, for example, look quite like the adults and are called *nymphs*. Crabs, starfishes and many other water-dwelling invertebrates pass through larval stages, but the only vertebrate (backboned) animals with larvae are the amphibians, the frogs, toads, newts and their relatives. Their larvae live in water and are called tadpoles.

The change from larva to adult is called METAMORPHOSIS. Insect larvae first turn into pupae or chrysalises and while they are in this stage their bodies gradually change

▶ *Caterpillars and other insect larvae (grubs) have the same basic design, but the adults are very different in appearance. Jellyfish larvae already have the characteristic shape of the adult.*

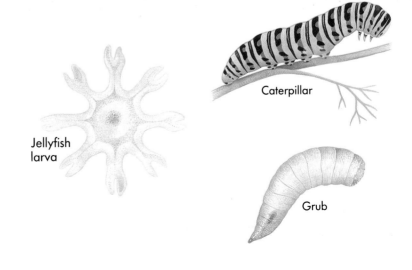

Caterpillar

Jellyfish larva

Grub

to the adult form. Other organisms change from larvae into a form very similar to a small adult which then grows into a full-sized adult.

Laser

A laser is a device that produces an intense beam of LIGHT. Laser light has only one WAVELENGTH and all the waves are in step with each other. The wavelength depends on the material used to make the laser. The word laser comes from Light Amplification by Stimulated Emission of Radiation, describing how a laser works. When an atom absorbs a unit of ENERGY called a PHOTON, it is said to be excited. If a second photon is fired at the excited atom, the extra energy is released as a burst of light (stimulated emission of radiation).

The first lasers used a ruby crystal excited by a powerful flash of light. As ruby lasers produce brief flashes or pulses of laser light, they are described as *pulse lasers*.

Theodore Maiman (1927–)
The United States physicist Theodore Maiman constructed the first working laser in 1960. After developing the maser (a device that generates or amplifies microwaves) in 1955 he began to work on an optical maser, or laser. His device consisted of a cylindrical artificial ruby crystal with parallel mirror-coated ends, one of which was semi-transparent. Bursts of intense white light were provided by a flash lamp.

◄ A laser beam is being used to check the alignment of a tunnel under construction. This makes use of the fact that laser light does not spread out as ordinary light does.

◄ Lasers do not generate light, they amplify it. Inside a laser, light from an external source is trapped between semi-silvered mirrors. The light is reflected to and fro through an energized crystal or gas. The atoms in the crystal or gas absorb photons of light and become excited. When struck by other photons, the atoms release light energy. All the light produced is of exactly the same frequency, and is therefore known as coherent light.

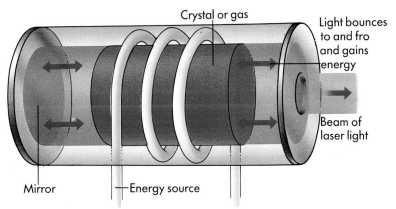

Crystal or gas

Light bounces to and fro and gains energy

Beam of laser light

Mirror

Energy source

▲ *Lasers are used in shops to read bar codes. Each item in the shop will have a bar code. When an item is sold the laser at the check-out till reads the bar code and registers the selling price at the till and on the bill. The information will also be passed on to a central database so that levels of stock in the shop can be monitored.*

▶ *The surface of a laser disc, magnified 100 times. Laser discs allow large amounts of information to be stored in a small area. A compact disc has a total track length of 57 kilometres. Thirty tracks are as wide as a human hair. A 120 mm compact disc will hold 74 minutes of programming.*

During the recording of a compact disc, each second of sound is broken up by a computer into 44,100 samples. The tiny samples are converted into a digital code. This code is cut by a laser into the master compact disc as millions of microscopic pits.

Gas lasers produce a continuous beam of light from a tube filled with gases such as argon, carbon dioxide or a mixture of helium and neon. Lasers have many uses. Some are used to perform delicate surgical operations on a human eye. More powerful lasers can cut through concrete or steel.

See also HOLOGRAM; MASER.

Laser disc

A laser disc is a disc used to record SOUND or pictures or sometimes both as a pattern of dull spots on a shiny metallic background. The disc is played by shining a LASER beam on the disc as it spins at high speed. The beam reflects off the shiny metal surface back into a detector. It does not reflect into the detector from the dull spots which are tiny holes or pits burned into the disc when the recording was made. The flashing reflections picked up by the detector produce a series of DIGITAL electrical

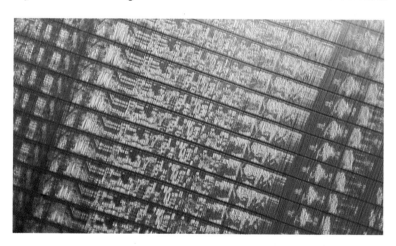

pulses at the rate of over 44,000 per second. These are decoded by the player's ELECTRONICS and changed back into the original sound or pictures that were recorded on the disc. Laser discs can store sound only (compact discs), vision and sound (VIDEO discs) or COMPUTER data.

Latent heat

Latent heat is the amount of HEAT energy that is absorbed or given out without causing a change in TEMPERATURE when a substance undergoes a change of state, for example, from a SOLID to a LIQUID or from a liquid to a GAS. Latent heat changes the state of a substance with-

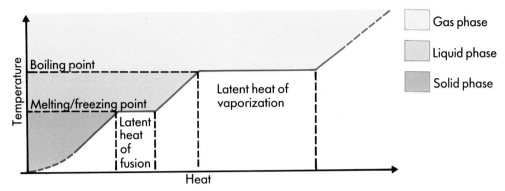

out altering the substance's temperature. For example, a kettle boils at 100°C, and this temperature remains constant until all the water has turned to water vapour. The extra heat or energy applied to the water in the kettle is used to change the water to water vapour.

In the change from solid to liquid and liquid to vapour, heat ENERGY is absorbed. In the reverse processes, when liquids freeze and become solids or gases condense into liquids, heat is given out.

▲ A change of physical state is also called a phase change. During a phase change, such as melting or freezing, a substance loses or absorbs heat without altering its temperature. Latent heat is the energy lost or gained during a phase change.

Lathe

A lathe is a MACHINE used to shape wood or metal in which the object to be shaped spins against a tool which does the shaping. The cutting tool is pushed against the spinning work-piece to shave away unwanted material. This is called turning. For wood turning, the tools may be held by hand and steadied against a tool-rest. For metal turning, the cutting tools are clamped to a moving platform controlled by two hand-wheels.

A lathe can be used for drilling, polishing and cutting screw threads into metal rods. On some lathes, the motor speed and tool position can be precisely controlled by computer.

▲ A modern lathe can create an artificial hip joint from information fed into it by a computer. Accurate drawings of the joint are first made on a computer and the information about the dimensions fed directly into the lathe.

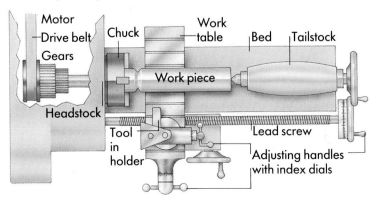

◄ Accurate machining on a lathe requires very precise adjustments to the angle of the cutting tool and the speed of rotation of the lathe.

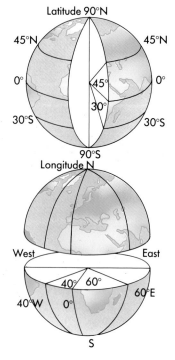

▲ *Latitude is measured by degrees north or south of the equator; longitude, by degrees east or west of the Greenwich meridian. Each degree is divided into 60 minutes.*

▼ *Any point on the Earth's surface can be given a position by using latitude and longitude, for example: Rio de Janeiro – 23°S, 43°W; Dakar – 14°N, 17°W; and London – 51°N, 0°.*

Latitude and Longitude

Latitude is the distance North or South of the equator, measured as an angle, of any point on the globe of the EARTH's surface. Thus, the equator is 0° while the North Pole is 90° North, and the South Pole is 90° South. For navigation and map-making, imaginary lines may be drawn on the globe parallel to each other and to the equator. These are known as lines of latitude.

A *meridian* is an imaginary circle drawn around the globe which passes through the North and South Poles. Longitude is the distance East or West of one particular meridian, the Greenwich Meridian, measured as an angle. In 1880 an international agreement was established that the meridian from which longitude is measured should be the one which passes through Greenwich Observatory in south-east London, England. Thus, this line of longitude is 0° while any point on this line of longitude on the opposite side of the globe is 180° and the longitude of all other points are given as an angle between 0° and 180° East or West of the Greenwich meridian.

SEE FOR YOURSELF
Wax behaves in the same way as magma and lava. Place a candle in sunlight for an hour or so, then handle it to see how it has softened. At higher temperatures, such as those produced by a candle flame, the wax flows like water, but quickly hardens.

Lava

Lava is the molten ROCK which spews out from a VOLCANO or some other kind of volcanic vent. If the lava contains a lot of dissolved gas, it may be frothy in character and may flow very rapidly. Pumice stone, which some people use to remove rough skin, is a kind of cooled lava which was so gassy that it is light enough to float on water. Some kinds of lavas are thick and treacly, and will only flow slowly. Some lavas are glassy whereas others contain large CRYSTALS of MINERALS. Some IGNEOUS ROCKS are formed as lavas.

Sometimes, a lava flow may happen so suddenly and so quickly that large areas of land may be engulfed almost without warning. In 1961 the inhabitants of Tristan da Cunha in the South Atlantic were evacuated to escape from fast flowing lava.

Lavoisier, Antoine *See Chemistry*

Lead

Lead is a soft heavy bluish-grey metallic ELEMENT which has many uses. It is used in the building and roofing trades, in the chemical industry, in building nuclear reactors, in making lead-acid storage batteries and high-quality glass, and in the oil industry. Lead can be easily hammered into flat sheets, cut with a knife, bent into different shapes and drawn out into thin wires, but it cannot conduct ELECTRICITY well. Lead is very resistant to CORROSION by moisture or ACIDS and is often used as a protective covering. Lead cannot be expelled from the body and a build-up of too much of the metal leads to lead poisoning. Lead can therefore cause serious pollution and so people are increasingly converting their cars to run on lead-free petrol, and replacing lead pipes with copper or plastic ones.

▲ *Lava emerges from the earth at temperatures between 800 and 1200°C. A lava flow may travel up to 10 km but as it flows it becomes cooler and slows down, until it finally solidifies.*

Lead's chemical symbol Pb comes from *plumbum*, the Latin word for waterworks. This is because lead was used to make the ancient Roman waterpipes. The Roman writer Plinius describes a disease among the slaves who extracted the lead that is clearly lead poisoning.

◀ *Most of the world's lead comes from Australia, the U.S. and China, where it is mined as the ores galena and cerusite.*

Ivan Pavlov (1849–1936)
Pavlov was a Russian biologist who was the first to make a scientific study of learning by association. He worked with dogs and noticed how their saliva began to run every time they were fed. This was a normal reflex action – the dogs did not have to think about it. Then Pavlov rang a bell every time the dogs were fed. After a while, he saw that the dogs' saliva began to run as soon as they heard the bell – even before the food arrived. The dogs had learned to associate the sound of the bell with food. Pavlov called this type of reaction a conditioned reflex.

▶ *Many animals can be trained to perform certain tasks or tricks. Offering rewards is an effective way of encouraging the animal to learn.*

Between 10 and 15 percent of children between the ages of 5 and 17 have one or more learning disabilities. These children may have average or above-average intelligence.

Learning

All animals are born with the ability to do certain things, but they soon begin to learn new things or to improve their inborn actions. Even earthworms can learn. If the worms are made to crawl along a forked tube and are given a mild electric shock in one arm of the fork they soon learn to take the other arm, and they can remember this for several days. This is an example of learning by trial and error. Many animals learn about food in this way. They instinctively peck at anything when they are young, but they soon discover which things are edible and which things are not. Birds and mammals learn a lot from their parents, by watching how they hunt or gather food and seeing just what kinds of food they bring home. Learning by association, which is also called *conditioning*, is another important learning method. If an

animal regularly finds food in a particular place or habitat it is likely to associate the two things and to visit the place when it is hungry. It will have a good chance of finding food there.

See also BEHAVIOUR; INSTINCT; INTELLIGENCE.

Leaves

Leaves are often called food factories, for it is in the leaves that green plants make most of their food, by PHOTOSYNTHESIS. A typical leaf has a thin blade called the lamina on a slender stalk called the petiole. The leaf cells are packed with chloroplasts which contain CHLORO-

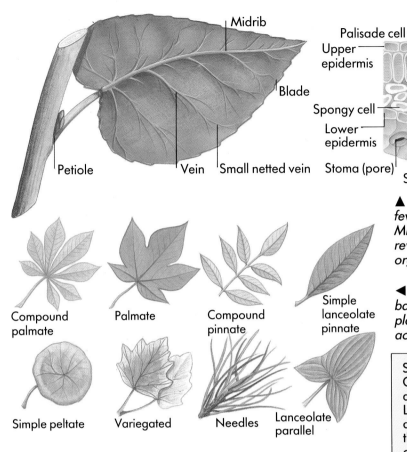

Midrib

Blade

Petiole

Vein

Small netted vein

Palisade cell

Upper epidermis

Chloroplasts

Spongy cell

Lower epidermis

Stoma (pore)

Supporting fibres

▲ *To the naked eye, a leaf has few interesting features. Microscopic examination reveals the complex organization of leaf tissue.*

◄ *There are fewer than ten basic designs for leaves, so plants are sometimes classified according to leaf-shape.*

Compound palmate

Palmate

Compound pinnate

Simple lanceolate pinnate

Simple peltate

Variegated

Needles

Lanceolate parallel

PHYLL, the green PIGMENT at the heart of the photosynthetic process. Water needed for photosynthesis is carried to the veins, which also carry away the food produced. Microscopic holes called stomata are found mainly on the underside of the leaf. Excess water escapes through these holes and oxygen and carbon dioxide can pass through them too. Plants living in very dry places usually have small leaves with few stomata, so that they do not lose too much water and wilt.

A leaf does not live for more than a few years because the chlorophyll breaks down and the leaf can no longer make food. Even evergreen trees have to renew their leaves, although they do not replace them all at once. Deciduous trees drop their leaves every year, usually in the autumn. Before they fall the leaves often take on brilliant colours.

See also TRANSPIRATION.

Leclanché cèll *See* Battery

Leeuwenhoek, Anton van *See* Microscope

SEE FOR YOURSELF
Collect leaves from as many different plants as you can find. Look carefully at their shapes, are they a cluster of leaves, are they all one colour. You can classify them according to the shapes shown above.

**Augustine Fresnel
(1788–1827)**
Fresnel was a French
physicist who developed the
transverse-wave theory of
light, as a result of his work
on lenses and optical
interference. Fresnel showed
that normal sunlight consisted
of vibrations that were at right
angles (transverse) to the
direction travelled by the
light. He also invented a type
of lens in which the surface is
cut into a series of concentric
steps rising towards the
centre. These lenses are still
widely used in lighthouses.

Lens, optical

An optical lens is a device for changing the shape and
direction of a beam of LIGHT. It works by using the process of REFRACTION, which causes the direction of a wave
to change when it passes from one material to another.
The speed of light waves in ordinary glass is only about
three quarters of their speed in air, so light can be bent
when it passes from air into glass and out again. Glass, or
transparent plastic, lenses are made in two different
sorts of shapes, concave and convex; a concave lens
bends the light which passes through it outwards away
from the centre, while a convex lens deflects the light
inwards. The place at which the beam of light is brought
together at a single point is called the FOCUS of the lens;
the distance of the focus from the lens itself is called the
focal length of the lens.

Our EYES have lenses which focus all the light reach-
ing them from a particular object onto a single point on
the retina at the back of the eye. The focal length of the
lens can be adjusted because the lens is flexible and its
shape can be changed by the surrounding MUSCLES; this
enables the eye to focus on objects at different distances.
The glass lens which does the same job in a camera is not
flexible and has to be moved in order to focus and so
allow photographs to be taken at different distances.
See also MICROSCOPE; TELESCOPE.

▶ *A convex lens produces a
real image (which can be
projected onto a screen), on
the opposite side of the lens.
The image is usually smaller
than the object and is inverted.
A concave lens produces a
virtual image (which can be
seen between the object and
the lens, but which cannot be
projected). The image is the
right way up, but it is smaller.
Most optical instruments use a
combination of convex and
concave lenses to produce an
image that is bright and in
focus.*

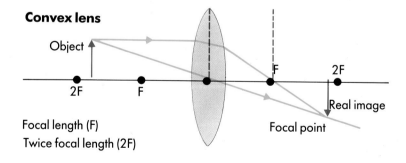

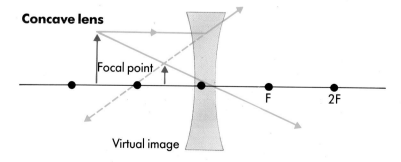